The Inner Nazi

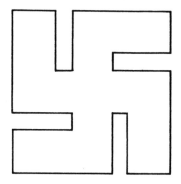

A Critical Analysis

Edited, with an Introduction
and a Biographical Afterword,
by Peter M. Rutkoff
and William B. Scott

The Inner Nazi

of MEIN KAMPF

HANS STAUDINGER

Louisiana State University Press
Baton Rouge and London

Designer: Albert Crochet
Typeface: VIP Trump Medieval
Typesetter: G & S Typesetters, Inc.

Portions of the Editors' Introduction first appeared in the
Annals of Scholarship. The editors are grateful for permis-
sion to reprint the material.
The editors are also grateful for permission to use extensive
quotations from *Mein Kampf* by Adolf Hitler (Complete and
Unabridged Edition/ Fully Annotated, published by Reynal
& Hitchcock in arrangement with Houghton Mifflin Com-
pany). Copyright, 1939 and Copyright © renewed 1967, by
Houghton Mifflin Company. Reprinted by permission of
Houghton Mifflin Company.

LIBRARY OF CONGRESS CATALOGING IN PUBLICATION DATA

Staudinger, Hans, 1889–
  The inner Nazi.

  1. Hitler, Adolf, 1889–1945. Mein Kampf.
2. National socialism. I. Rutkoff, Peter M., 1942–
II. Scott, William B., 1945–   . III. Title.
DD247.H5A3583   943.085′092′4   81-7277
ISBN 0-8071-0882-0   AACR2

To the Graduate Faculty of
the New School for Social Research

Contents

Acknowledgments

Hans Staudinger's generosity, warmth, and patience during our search for historical truth were the ingredients that made publication of this book possible. We would like, as well, to thank Elizabeth Todd Staudinger for her permission to edit her husband's work. Mary Sparlin at Kenyon College typed and retyped. We thank her also. Beverly Jarrett and Judy Bailey at Louisiana State University Press provided help, discipline, and courage when we needed it. Without them this project would have remained unpublished. As we remember Hans Staudinger we are sure he would have given much credit to his assistant at the graduate faculty, Werner Pese.

The Inner Nazi

Editors' Introduction

"You have to know Hitler. I knew him. I hated him," declared Hans Staudinger in a 1978 interview.[1] Prior to World War I, as a graduate student, Staudinger had studied with Max and Alfred Weber at Heidelberg University where he received his doctorate. After the war he served as state secretary in the Prussian Ministry of Trade and Commerce and was subsequently elected to the Reichstag as a Social Democrat. His socialist affiliation made Staudinger an early target of the Nazis. In 1933 he managed to escape from Germany and accepted a professorship of economics at the newly organized "University in Exile" in New York City. The University in Exile was founded by Alvin Johnson, president of the New School for Social Research, to provide an academic shelter for European scholars who had fled Hitler. Staudinger later became dean of the Graduate Faculty of the New School, the successor to the University in Exile. In 1938 Staudinger began to translate *Mein Kampf*, a work which he believed was critical to an understanding of the inner motives of Hitler's Germany. Two years later he published an analysis of the economy of the Third Reich, "The Future of Totalitarian Barter Trade Economy," which appeared in *Social Research*.[2] In 1941 Staudinger, with the assistance of Werner Pese, a research associ-

1. Hans Staudinger, Interview II, November 19, 1978.
2. Hans Staudinger, "The Future of Totalitarian Barter Trade Economy," *Social Research*, VII (1940), 410–29.

ate, started to write *The Inner Nazi*. Never before published, *The Inner Nazi* represents the analysis of Nazi ideology by a person who intimately knew and participated in the events that brought Hitler to power.

Between September, 1978, and May, 1979, we interviewed Staudinger approximately a dozen times. At first he was formal, graciously correct yet suspicious. For him it was imperative that we understand first things first: the reasons for the New School's existence and direction, the critical and special contribution of Alvin Johnson in the rescue of a generation of émigré intellectuals, and finally, above all else, Staudinger's own wariness of being misunderstood. Too many errors had been made in the past, and he did not want them repeated.

So we sat, three or four hours at a time, taking notes. Staudinger's white-maned and handsomely chiseled head leaned over our shoulders to insure that our notes were accurate. He pointed his finger for emphasis. Gradually, his mistrust gave way to trust and trust to friendship. Then in December, 1978, two conversations transpired that led to the eventual discovery and publication of the text of *The Inner Nazi*.

By that time we had succeeded in uncovering in the basement boiler room of the New School's Twelfth Street building an archive of miscellaneous records and papers that had managed to survive periodic housecleaning efforts. Among the unorganized array of boxes, files, reports, and reprints, we discovered, almost intact, the papers of the New School's research division, the Institute for World Affairs. The institute, directed by the theoretical economist Adolph Lowe, functioned from 1942 to 1953 to research questions of public policy, particularly questions of postwar economic, political, and social reconstruction. It was created, as well, as a haven for dozens of European-trained social scientists who would have otherwise found little or no academic employment. Staudinger served as chairman of the institute's Research Council

(1943–1950) and as its director (1950–1953). Almost single-handedly he arranged for its initial funding in one evening in 1942 when he persuaded the Doris Duke Foundation to contribute a half million dollars to the institute. The Duke Foundation money also enabled the New School itself to avoid bankruptcy proceedings that had already been initiated. This was the first but not the last time Staudinger's abilities as a fund raiser saved the New School and the Graduate Faculty from financial disaster.

Among the papers of the Institute of World Affairs, we found a leisure-time project that Staudinger had directed between 1947 and 1950 but had never completed. "The Leisure-Time Study" initiated Staudinger's lifelong interest in the possible cultural autonomy of the working classes as a basis for a socialist political community. Staudinger had investigated the issue as a doctoral student at Heidelberg University and following World War I had tried to implement it as a German and Prussian civil servant and then as a Social Democratic member of the Reichstag from 1932 to 1933.

At our next interview in early December, 1978, we questioned Staudinger about the project. He recounted his graduate training with Max and Alfred Weber and revealed what at first seemed to be traces of social and cultural conservatism inconsistent with his socialism. Staudinger recalled in words almost identical to those contained in a 1947 memo that he had hoped to continue his work as doctoral student prior to World War I but that, finally, he had decided to abandon the project. "I'll tell you why," he said slowly and painfully. "I could not bear the tentative conclusions. They showed that as human beings we lead dissatisfied and unreflective lives."[3] The intensity of his response was startling.

Two weeks later, Staudinger phoned and said, "I have some-

---

3. Staudinger, Interview IV, December 22, 1978.

thing important to show you." When we arrived at his apartment, he handed us a manuscript entitled *The Inner Nazi*, which he thought we might find interesting. He had kept the manuscript in his study and had only once, in late 1943 or early 1944, considered publication. Like the leisure study it had remained unpublished. Yet, unlike the leisure project, *The Inner Nazi* had been completed and had remained in Staudinger's personal possession. When Staudinger wrote *The Inner Nazi* (1941–1943), he was seeking to answer the question that puzzled so many of his contemporaries: What was the nature and significance of Nazism? "It was," said one of his colleagues, "the task of our entire generation to make known the real meaning of Nazism to an America still saturated with isolationism.[4] Even so, Staudinger apparently cared little about publication. He was content to remain a leader of his colleagues. His appointment as the first permanent dean of the Graduate Faculty (1952–1959) was based on his willingness to act while permitting others to take public credit.

Staudinger completed *The Inner Nazi* in 1943 or early 1944.[5] He presented the completed version to Alvin Johnson for possible publication in *Social Research*, the scholarly journal sponsored by the University in Exile. Staudinger recalled that one Friday afternoon he gave Johnson the manuscript along with several bottles of Moselle wine. Johnson promised to finish both over the weekend. A notoriously slow reader, Johnson did not return to his office until the following Wednesday. According to Staudinger, Johnson had become "magnetized" by the manuscript and wanted to devote the entire next issue of *Social Research* to *The Inner Nazi*. Staudinger recalled being pleased at Johnson's enthusiasm but puzzled at the "magnetic" appeal. Johnson explained that while he understood

4. Henry Pachter, Interview, March, 1979.
5. Staudinger, Interview VIII, April 27, 1979.

Staudinger's description of Hitler as truly evil, he nonetheless felt strangely drawn by the power of the appeal itself. While he was not flirting with Nazi thought, for the first time Johnson said that he understood its incredible ideological attraction. Staudinger remembered his shock. Johnson was hardly a naïve man. But "the Nazis were our enemy. We hated them. It could not be permitted that my book might somehow gain that enemy any admiration."[6] If Johnson could be "attracted," how might others react? Despite Johnson's insistence that the manuscript be published, Staudinger concluded that if its message were misunderstood, it might result in sympathy for the Nazi cause. Thirty-five years later, shortly before his death, Staudinger finally consented to the publication of *The Inner Nazi*, certain at last that he would not be misunderstood.

Staudinger's stylistic format was, indeed, apt to mislead the reader. Staudinger believed that the force and texture of Hitler's ideas could only be conveyed through lengthy quotations from Hitler's speeches and writings, particularly *Mein Kampf*. *The Inner Nazi* is thus, in part, a documentary history of Hitler's thought as Staudinger allowed Hitler to speak for himself. It is an essay within an essay. In each chapter Staudinger bracketed Hitler's words between an editorial introduction and a conclusion, with an occasional editorial explanation within the quoted text itself. To convey the immediacy of the events, Staudinger throughout the manuscript adopted the present tense. At times it was difficult for readers to distinguish Staudinger's interpretive comments from Hitler's assertive statements. As originally written, *The Inner Nazi* almost invited the misunderstanding Staudinger had sought to avoid. Only the most careful reader could keep the author (Staudinger) separate at all times from his subject (Hitler). With Stau-

6. Staudinger, Interview VII, March 15, 1979.

dinger's permission and on the advice of outside readers, we have clarified the text by putting Staudinger's comments in the past tense while leaving Hitler's statements or Staudinger's paraphrasing of them in the present. To facilitate reading, we have also editorially corrected some of Staudinger's English prose and syntax, again with the author's permission. In all instances the original meaning has been scrupulously preserved.

Despite the risk of misunderstanding, Staudinger's documentary format makes *The Inner Nazi* a particularly effective document. Clearly and in his own words, Hitler is presented to English readers. At the same time, Staudinger, Hitler's Social Democratic opponent, presents himself in his editorial commentary. *The Inner Nazi* is, thus, two documents: one of Hitler, the ruler of Germany, and another of Hans Staudinger, the exiled Weimar civil servant. *The Inner Nazi* is a confrontation between the Nazi Hitler and the Social Democrat Staudinger. Even as he acknowledged Hitler's ascendency in Germany, Staudinger expected to have the last word as he looked forward to a reconstructed Germany purged of nazism. Staudinger considered himself both observer/social scientist and participant/politician. For this reason *The Inner Nazi* is as interesting for what it reveals about Staudinger as for what it has to say about Hitler.

Staudinger's analysis represents an interpretation of nazism that informed his political behavior as a Weimar politician and civil servant and that retains, a generation after its writing, much of its explanatory power. Staudinger understood that the "crackpot" and his "motley crew" meant to accomplish exactly what they said they would. The Nazis were neither opportunists nor ad hoc radicals. Rather, starting with Hitler, they took the racist ideology of *Mein Kampf* seriously and intended, had always intended, to fulfill the ideological goals of the movement. Staudinger was surprised neither by the outbreak of war in 1939 nor by the Russian invasion of 1941. Although horrified by the "final solution," he saw it as the manifest conclusion of *Mein Kampf*. Similarly, Staudinger's appreciation of the extent to which Nazi ideology successfully permeated German society forced him to conclude that the Nazi problem was a German problem.

The Inner Nazi stands apart from most other contemporary accounts of nazism in its lack of clear ideological bias. *The Inner Nazi* is an interpretation of Hitler's political power by a preeminently political man whose criteria were rooted in his practical and intellectual experiences. Staudinger's text betrays few of the explicitly radical or conservative attitudes that characterize many other contemporary accounts. In contrast to Franz Neumann's classic study, *Behemoth*, Staudinger in *The Inner Nazi* argued that Hitler's ideology, far more powerfully than German society, determined the evolution of the Nazi state. Neumann concentrated on the social and economic continuities between the Weimar Republic and the Third Reich, insisting that the Nazis did not fundamentally alter the German social structure, and Staudinger did not dispute him. In his article on totalitarian barter trade, Staudinger even argued that in economic policy the Nazis merely extended the "neo-mercantilist" practices that he and other state planners had developed in Germany and Prussia between 1923 and 1933. Staudinger saw that it was the "state as entrepreneur" both before and after 1933 that was the agent for economic and, subsequently, political domination.[7] Using strategies of price-fixing and alternative production to shift output from consumer goods to heavy armament industries, the Nazis created a European economic *Gleichschaltung* on

7. Franz Neumann, *Behemoth: The Structure and Practice of National Socialism* (New York: 1944); Staudinger, "Future of Totalitarian Barter Trade."

the heels of which marched political hegemony. This operation, insisted Staudinger, was neither profitable in economic terms nor beneficial politically to the private capitalist-industrialist. The state in Weimar and the party-state in the Third Reich planned and executed these economic maneuvers for their own, though quite different, political ends. The German industrial-finance capitalist was not strengthened by Nazi economic and political activities.

Staudinger challenged Neumann's concept of working-class isolation and political immunity from the capitalist producer and, subsequently, from the Nazi state and ideology. Instead, Staudinger suggested that Nazi ideology became a part of German culture, affecting all strata of the society. Indeed, his insistence on systematic postwar denazification was the final chapter in Staudinger's understanding of the relationship between the working class and socialism, trade unionism, and nazism. To this issue, which involved a special appreciation of the failures of German socialism, Staudinger brings a fresh perspective born of personal involvement.

Staudinger argued that the divisions between the Socialist party and the trade unions were so severe that the working class, especially after 1927, found itself unable to respond to the succession of economic and political crises that hammered the Weimar Republic. The Socialist–trade union schism was resolved by the victory of the unions that chose to support the private capitalist economy. For Staudinger the real failure was the inability of the Socialists to gain working-class adherence to the ideas and policies of state planning and an "organized economy." Consequently, Staudinger's Socialist colleagues in their preoccupation with the internecine debate within the left itself failed to recognize the threat from the right. "I told [Rudolf] Hilferding [prominent member of SPD] in 1927 that he had to read *Mein Kampf*," Staudinger disclosed in a recent interview. "He said that he couldn't stand more than ten minutes of that garbage."[8]

More importantly, Staudinger believed that the Nazis profited from the inability of the Social Democrats to incorporate the working class, through the trade unions, into their own political program. His understanding represented a kind of equation, a physics of social ideologies. What German socialism failed to accomplish or failed to provide for the working class, German National Socialism was able to promise. In the context of political and economic crisis, the Nazis found first the lower middle and then the working classes susceptible to their ideological pitch. In *The Inner Nazi* Staudinger developed this interpretation by stressing the consistency of the ideological appeal in combination with its cultural and social pervasiveness. Unlike Neumann, Staudinger clearly perceived and established the role and function of racist ideology in the Third Reich, identified the state as the monopolistic entrepreneur engaged in a process of economic and political domination, and described the relationship between Nazi theory and practice.

If Staudinger could not accept the characterization of nazism as solely an extension and reinforcement of Weimar's class and economic structure, neither did he view it as inevitable and in some sense necessary given the "crisis of modernity." In short, he rejected the pessimistic and explicitly conservative interpretation of persons such as F. R. Reck-Malleczewen in *The Diary of a Man in Despair.*[9]

For Reck-Malleczewen, Hitler's Germany represented the culmination of "modernity." The victory of Hitler and "his

8. Jehuda Riemer, Interview, July 25, 1978; Staudinger to "friend" Hennis, May 12, 1977, in the Archives of the Graduate Faculty of the New School for Social Research, New York City; Staudinger, Interview II.
9. F. R . Reck-Malleczewen, *Diary of a Man in Despair* (New York: 1971).

gang" was the necessary consequence of the dismantlement of the Christian, hierarchical, rurally based social order of pre-Bismarckian Germany. Reck-Malleczewen despaired not only over the Nazis' claim to represent the "new" or "heroic" in the midst of mechanical mediocrity but also over their uncivilized and uncultured means of asserting the claim. As a result, the only intellectual response for Reck-Malleczewen was an almost apocalyptical hope for the annihilation of all changes since the Renaissance.

The victory of national socialism had no such lessons for Staudinger. Rather, as he made clear in *The Inner Nazi*, the specific circumstances of crisis and the response of Hitler explain the origins of the Third Reich. Staudinger accounted for the "icy darkness" that descended upon Germany by the failures not of "modernity" but of those who should have defended it, the Social Democrats.[10] Thus, he understood the Nazi victory as evidence of political failure rather than cultural decadence or working-class alienation. The inevitable war that was a consequence of this failure, Staudinger argued, stemmed from the racist component expressed in *Mein Kampf*, the search for "living space" dictating military conquest to the east. The particular conduct of the war and the policy of racial extermination were parallel results of the same ideological impulse. *The Inner Nazi*, while sharing some of the perspective of *Behemoth* on the one hand and *The Diary of a Man in Despair* on the other, is a document that reveals the fundamental political, but not ideological, judgment of its author. Staudinger, too, saw the economic continuities with Weimar as he understood the significance of the social origins of the Nazi leaders. But he found both Reck-Malleczewen's conservative and Neumann's neo-Marxist interpretations inadequate.

10. Staudinger, Interview IV, December 22, 1978.

another purpose

✗   Staudinger hoped to make postwar policy makers aware of
the intrinsically evil character of Nazi ideology so that they
would root it out of German culture. But concerned that English readers might become "magnetized" rather than re-
pulsed, Staudinger chose to remain silent. Ironically, because
developments in postwar Germany have fulfilled many of
Staudinger's hopes, much of the present value of *The Inner
Nazi* is due to the insights it provides into Hans Staudinger.
Staudinger's analysis of German society and his critique of
nazism reveals a facet of German culture and politics that, in
the 1930s and 1940s, Hitler's presence overshadowed. Staudinger personified the effort by numerous Germans in the
1920s to bring economic and political democracy to Germany.
Because of a number of factors, many beyond their control,
they failed. But if the democratic and peaceful character of
West Germany persists, in time we may come to see Adolf
Hitler, not Hans Staudinger, as the historical aberration. To
understand German culture we will need to examine Weber
and Brecht rather than Nietzsche and Wagner.

1 卐 The Power of an Idea

To know the enemy is one means to victory. Yet an insight into his military strength alone will not suffice. Not the billions of tons of munitions will be decisive in this war, but instead, the human reserves and the will to make the utmost use of fighting potentialities. *Knowing* refers to the *ideas* that engendered the dynamics for expansion leading to this war, that still give—we may not like to believe it—the enormous impetus to so many leaders and warriors in the German home and fighting fronts. *Knowing* intends to reveal nothing less than the true war aims—namely, aims for which Hitler and his inner circle are striving and fighting.

This does not mean to indulge in jugglery and speculations on what are to be the specific war aims with regard to the frontiers of Nazi Europe. Whatever the various groups of the Nazis and the military and governmental bureaucracy may think with regard to the future set-up of the countries in Europe is anybody's guess. If one wants to consider Nazi behavior in the face of the present European situation, one had better concentrate on studies of the economic and political changes already wrought by Hitler's oppression of all European peoples and the ruthless extinction of the former structure of the society of many peoples. Such studies may reveal the extent of the resistance of the oppressed peoples and may indicate Germany's reserves and resources through the further possible exploitation of Europe. Certainly, it is important that such studies be made in order to show the economic and social interrelations and ties among European peoples, which cannot be so easily dissolved into their former relations after the war without further endangering the already low standard of living of European countries. Yet however useful such studies, they too fail to say much about what the Nazis have in mind with their "new order in Europe."

 The Nazi new order of Europe can be understood only within the framework of the total picture of Hitler's expansionist ideas. In essence, these are worldwide goals for which the Nazis are fighting. It would be utter folly to believe that Nazi conquest receives its impetus from nothing but bloodthirst and a power obsession. The convinced Nazis are certainly not facile opportunists. Hitler and a large group of his influential followers do not plan conquest solely for the selfish purpose of keeping themselves in power. If that were true, they could have stopped at Munich for their own benefit and security; they could have enjoyed an enormous power position at home and abroad. But there is an inescapable force behind their further actions that, unleashed within themselves, carried them forward.

It has been said that government and military leaders could have stemmed the tide of the stirred-up Nazi party. According to this view, it was the dynamics of the Nazi movement as such that had automatically precipitated Germany into the war venture against Poland. It is true that the Nazis considered the diplomatic success of Hitler in Munich a shameful setback; in many cities of Germany they pulled down the flags that had been hoisted in celebration of Munich. Such tragedies have often occurred throughout the course of history. Responsible governments have gone reluctantly to war, compelled by the whipped-up, war-fevered masses or sometimes by the military machine once set into motion. Yet the outbreak of the World War (1939–) was not the result of the overcharged war atmosphere seeking for release, nor of the unrolling of the power-thirsty Nazi machine. It was Hitler himself and his closer advisors who, according to their long-standing plan, threw the German armies into Poland. This third invasion (after Austria and Czechoslovakia) was one of the steps necessitated by their final goals.

We must distinguish clearly between the variegated Nazi war plans for new frontiers in Europe. Hitler's goals are: a greater Germany; a new order in Europe; and world domination by the Germans and Aryans, needed to fulfill their "mission" to create a new world culture such as the Nazis conceive it. One goal conditions the other, and the first is a function of the final. To understand this it is necessary to sift the concrete, day-by-day features of Nazi conquest from their underlying motives. To know the inner and somewhat hidden structure of this coming world means at the same time to know what is behind the impetus, the energy, and the sacrifices in blood.

There are many publications concerning Hitler that record stories, anecdotes, and conversations about him and the Nazis. It is strange though that none try to analyze thoroughly the Nazi world that was conceived in the minds of these ecstatic men. Yet this new world was already depicted in *Mein Kampf*. But until the war itself was well underway the Germans of the pre-Hitler period and others neglected to study thoroughly Hitler's aims that led inevitably to war. In particular, Anglo-Saxon countries with their outspoken sense for concrete realities and pragmatic notions do not understand that there exists a revolutionary vision of a new inner structure of Europe in a new world. These countries have never been accustomed to view utopias as realities; they fail to make, so to say, a dissection of the Nazi mind. And that is imperative. Today such analyses of the mind of a young Nazi taking his training for the service of his Führer are even more necessary for warfare and for the future—the time to rebuild a distorted and destroyed world. Above all, such analyses make manifest to us the unbridgeable gulf between the Allied and the Axis causes.

Before going into an analysis of the Nazi war aims, we have to ask ourselves whether we are right to regard *Mein Kampf* as an authentic and correct basis for Hitler's total system from which these ends emanated. An Adolf Hitler of the early twenties published *Mein Kampf* at a time when he was a nobody, a man who had been defeated in a ridiculous effort to seize power in a Beerhall Putch and had been disposed of by "honorary confinement" in a Bavarian fortress. At the time of his writings, Hitler was a man free of party ties and responsibilities; he could speak his mind frankly and had to consider no one's purposes but his own—void of reticence and ambiguity and not employing any of the diplomatic camouflage of his later days. At that time his words relied entirely upon their own weight; no political connections, no established party organization compelled him to become a tactician. Hitler's *Mein Kampf* is the work of a politically endowed visionary; it is not that of a politician.

We shall not enter the common debate concerning the relation of Hitler, as the author, to the content of *Mein Kampf*. Nor are we interested in whether he believed in his own words before he wrote them or whether he became "converted" by his own writings or was "converted" through intercourse with the thoughts of his contemporaries who later became his apostles and pacemakers in the political organizations. Nor shall we go into the question, whether *Mein Kampf* is the work of Hitler or is a collective work. For our inquiry *Mein Kampf* may be considered as an authentic and uncontaminated source because Hitler never deviated essen-

tially from the total vision he laid down in *Mein Kampf*. If in
his speeches and press releases he "corrected" or denied and
thus hid his real intentions, his actions nevertheless were
faithfully oriented by his ideas. His circle, too, wrote what
amounted more or less to commentaries on *Mein Kampf* that
filled in the vague and general outlines with concrete for-
mulations. Even if some, like Alfred Rosenberg, presented a
different emphasis in their motivations for Hitler's war aims,
the parallel to Hitler's basic system still prevails without im-
pinging on that system. Thus, we shall take this labyrinthine
book at its face value as properly expressing Hitler's system,
unadulterated by any external influences and opportunistic
tactics in its rational construction and its emotional self-
intoxication. The ideas made explicit in *Mein Kampf* have
guided and determined Nazi policy and activities from the beginning. In fact, they furnished inspiration for the movement
as early as the 1920s. In order to understand how they obtained such a hold, we must examine the way in which they
were communicated to the adherents, then how they could be
spread to the minds of the people.

In *Mein Kampf* Hitler stated that he did not intend to address the masses of the people with his book. He wished to
present his system to himself, to his friends, to the inner circle of his advisors, and to his small young party—a selected
few and a motley crew indeed. "With this work" he made
clear, "I do not address myself to strangers, but to those adherents of the movement who belong to it with their hearts
and whose reason now seeks a more intimate enlightenment.
I know that one is able to win people far more by the spoken
than by the written word, and that every great movement on
this globe owes its rise to the great speakers and not to the
great writers."[1]

1. Adolf Hitler, *Mein Kampf* (New York: Reynal and Hitchcock, 1939), xv,
hereinafter cited in the text by page number only.

Who were these first adherents and members of the movement, and why were they moved to "action" and to change of heart? They included young officers whose country did not provide a berth for them after the army had been dissolved according to the terms of the Versailles Treaty; members of the middle classes, expropriated by the process of German postwar inflation, whose social status in their communities was often undermined by the stronger political participation of the members of the working class; peasants hit by the long-lasting world agricultural depression; youths without hope of a job in a Germany filled with unemployed masses; and intellectuals and bureaucrats, who saw their ambitions frustrated by the manifold newcomers who represented the political views of the parties excluded from participation in the government during the Wilhelmian era. All these groups, living in an atmosphere of discontent created by the state of national humiliation following a lost war, the peace treaties, and social and economic hopelessness, furnished Hitler with adherents and members ready to gorge themselves on his teachings, to obey him blindly, and to carry his will to the people. Leadership in the party was taken by many white-collar workers and professionals who, unfamiliar with the complicated pattern of economic and social conditions, were willing to lend their frustrated minds to the new "gospel."

These adherents and members, endowed with his ideas and trained in the methods of fighting laid down in *Mein Kampf*, had the task of transferring Hitler's opinion to the masses to make voters and sympathizers out of them—in Hitler's nomenclature, "followers"—the fittest of whom could be recruited as party members.[2] In *Mein Kampf* Hitler defined followers and members, and stated their tasks: "If a movement

2. The word *follower* is used here in Hitler's specific sense as comprising also the "members" of the party, *i.e.*, the active and close adherents. In the introduction we have used *follower* in its specific sense.

has the intention of pulling down a world and of building a new one in its place, then there must be absolute clarity about the following points in the ranks of its own leaders: Every movement, at first, will have to divide the human material it has won into two great groups: into followers and members. The task of propaganda is to attract followers; the task of organization is to win members. A follower of a movement is one who declares himself in agreement with its aims; a member is one who fights for it" (849). He added, "The follower is inclined to like a movement by its propaganda. The member is induced by the organization to help personally towards acquiring new followers who then, in turn, can be trained to become members" (849).

It is one of the characteristics of Hitler's method that, with regard to the planning of his strategy, he worked with his closer circle of friends. When it came to political action, he worked with his party members. He involved the masses only in certain situations; for instance, before elections, in moments of political decision. At these times he organized meetings of the masses, flooded them with tabloids, newspapers, and pamphlet material; and he staged impressive parades of his special guards in order to attract and to stir up the onlookers. These meetings and parades, designed to create a highly emotional spirit, were brought to small towns and remote villages to gain new followers (voters and sympathizers) and to select from them new members of the party. Through these organizational and propaganda methods laid down in *Mein Kampf* even the farmers and middle-class people were, for the first time in recent German history, made politically conscious, and their growing participation in elections worked to Hitler's advantage. His party created new voters (followers), people who had never before exercised their franchise. The followers, too, belonged largely to the discontented sections of the people enumerated above.

It is the original and peculiar invention of Hitler that he offered his ideas in *Mein Kampf,* and simultaneously, he set up the organization with which to disseminate them, to make them effective. With this set-up, Hitler established the link between himself and the leading group, the acting forces and the masses, and created from the beginning of the movement a firm mutual interrelationship between those above and below—a plan that guaranteed action as well as continuous control of the followers.

I cannot sufficiently stress the social and economic conditions and the foreign political situation of Germany after the war and during the following inflation that created an atmosphere favorable for quacks and faith healers. It was the hopelessness, the incertitude of great numbers of the middle class and of the agricultural population throughout the twenties and culminating in the depression that led them into following a "leader." Furthermore, Hitler's personality cannot be overrated as a factor in building the Nazi movement. Even ministers of the Republic, like Wilhelm Gröner (Reich defense minister), felt Hitler's spell and termed him a "charismatic" and seductive leader of the German youth. Yet something more was needed to create the will for radical action in adherents and its echo in followers. Hitler, in *Mein Kampf,* gave to his party members a new "weltanschauung," with which these adherents indoctrinated ever-growing masses of sympathizers. Though primitive and unspecific, these new ideas were appealing because they offered a new, optimistic world view, which contained elements familiar to Germans in their former ideas of nation, national pride, and folk ideas. Such traditional ideals had been in the German mind for more than a hundred years; they constituted the object of intellectual discussions and political strife. They were certainly not invented by Hitler but were perverted and utilized under a specific political view. Hitler produced his *Weltbild* with great vision and invited the reader with imagination to put his own desires into it without having to dispute Hitler.

Hitler's system is in itself logically constructed. In its reasoning it is conclusive and compelling for the simple mind that does not question its assumptions nor its empirical and historical background. "Scientific" in form, biased in content, the German middle class took it at face value as "truth."[3] Though the terms of the system were "rationally" conceived, in their totality and in their conclusiveness the ideas possessed the emotional appeal and the compulsive character of a creed. Logical reasoning, by which Hitler's system is built up, turns, because of its conclusiveness, into an irrational belief system. In other words, because of its logical form, Germans believed that the system was true and that Hitler had arrived at the ultimate understanding of the workings of nature and history.

Hitler directed this new creed as embodied in *Mein Kampf* against Marxism, the creed of the German labor movement. As such, as a fighting instrument, it was practical and enticed its followers to "prepare for action" in a near future. Furthermore, Hitler's attacks on Jewish capitalism and appeals to the small and self-reliant businessman restored the self-confidence of a middle class badly in need of inspiration. The craftsmen, jealous of the workers whose relatively high wages and better hours were protected by the trade unions, felt that under national socialism a new time would come when they would be equal to or better than workingmen. All these people, whom

3. This does not mean that *Mein Kampf* can be regarded as a work of science. Its formal logical exposition undoubtedly appeared to many Germans as the sole criterion of science. However, Hitler's assumptions are given without thorough consideration of the studies and findings of modern social and natural scientists. The historical facts that he used as examples are interpreted without regard for the setting in which they occur but in the light of his unscrutinized, preconceived ideas.

the Marxist labor movement had necessarily left unmoved or had even alienated by its program to nationalize some forms of private enterprise, were ready to follow Hitler and his slogans—to become "conscious."

The Marxists also urged the workers to become conscious, but class consciousness was very different from the consciousness Hitler expected from his people. He had in mind racial and folk consciousness. In addition, Hitler's revolutionary slogans were "awake" and "act," while the labor movement in its growing tendency to subscribe to revisionist socialism taught that the economic evolution brought about by trial-and-error economic planning would gradually free the individual and the worker from the capitalist yoke. The socialist theory of a necessary and inevitable process of growth into a better future left little room for immediate action. Hitler's demand to "awake" was immediate. This immediateness was of great psychological importance. His millennium was to come tomorrow if only action were taken today. His promises held good not only for the future, not for the Great Beyond, but as well for a day that an emotionally aroused electorate felt to be close at hand. This conflux of will to act and hope of realization made for the spontaneity and the dynamic impetus of national socialism.

Hitler's ideas had this effect not only because of the organizational set-up of an active teacher-corps but also because of the technique of communication. Hitler called this specific technique of communication, described in *Mein Kampf*, propaganda, but it was quite different from the propaganda concept of the democracies. Hitler and his adherents or party members were aware that they had to present to the masses the "truth" of their own world in such positive terms that the slightest doubt could not arise even in a more critical mind. For Hitler, propaganda was a technique of black and white and the repetition of unchangeable stereotypes of which he and his adherents played up now the one, now the other. In order to arouse the Nazi brand of nationalism, the 100-percent-positive approach was strengthened by the 100-percent-negative criticism on the basis of the same utopian views. Nothing in the Weimar system was good; the Nazi members were prohibited from acknowledging even minor successes of the Weimar Republic. The Versailles system represented everything that was bad.

Hitler himself exploited Versailles as the focal propaganda instrument.

> In the boundlessness of its oppression [he declared], in the shamefulness of its demands, rests the greatest propaganda weapon for the rearousing of the dormant life spirits of a nation.
>
> But for that, of course, everything, beginning with the child's primer down to the last newspaper, every theater and every movie, every billboard and every bare wall, must be placed at the service of this single great mission, until the prayer of fear of our present-day parlor patriots, 'Lord deliver us!' changes in the mind of the smallest child to the burning plea: '*Almighty God, bless our arms; be just, as Thou always wert; judge now, whether we deserve freedom; Lord, bless our battle!*' (920–21)

The main ingredient of the recipe for this all-out propaganda is manipulation of the truth in favor of one side while fastening the blame on the other side. "Propaganda's task is," wrote Hitler,

> for instance, not to evaluate the various rights, but far more to stress exclusively the one that is to be represented by it. It has not to search into truth as far as this is favorable to others, in order to present it then to the masses with doctrinary honesty, but it has rather to serve its own truth uninterruptedly.
>
> It was fundamentally wrong to discuss the war guilt from the point of view that not Germany alone could be made responsible for the outbreak of this catastrophe, but it would have been far better to burden the enemy entirely with this guilt, even if this

had not been in accordance with the real facts, as was indeed the case. (236)

Hitler spoke of the realization of the idea by "the definite mutual interrelationship" between propaganda and organization:

> When propaganda has filled a whole people with an idea, the organization, with the help of a handful of people, can draw the consequences. Propaganda and organization—that means followers and members—have thus a definite mutual relationship. The better propaganda has been working, the smaller may be the organization. . . .
>
> The first task of propaganda is the winning of people for the future organization; the first task of the organization is the winning of people for the continuation of propaganda. The second task of propaganda is the destruction of the existing condition and the permeation of this condition with the new doctrine, while the second task of the organization must be the fight for power, so that by it it will achieve the final success of the doctrine. (851)[4]

* * *

The ideas embodied in *Mein Kampf* gave the élan to the Nazi movement, whatever external social and political factors may have contributed to its rapid spread. The taking over of the reins of government by Hitler had little or nothing directly to do with the ideas taught by him or even the more radical Nazi members. Only the fact that he was the leader of one of the largest parties and disposer of an enormous mass of voters made him the candidate for chancellorship. The right-wing parties, military and business groups, as well as some of the

4. Strictly speaking, and to follow Hitler's procedure, we have to keep apart, first, *ideas* in their existence as doctrines; second, *ideas in action, i.e.,* their transformation into propaganda and will to "fight for power"; third, *ideas in realization* in the minds of masses, *i.e.,* the power of the idea which makes "the community . . . ripe for the time of the victory of this idea" (850), so that Hitler, as the Führer of the Reich, would be able to objectivize the ideas into the new order in Germany and beyond.

political wire-pullers who finally convinced the aged Hinden-
burg to deliver up to Hitler the chairmanship of the Reichs-
cabinet, were utterly opposed to the main assumptions and
conclusions of the Nazi system. They despised Hitler and,
even more, the people who surrounded him, those "screw-
balls" whom he gathered together in the first actions at the
time of the Beerhall Putsch.

The conservative groups recognized that the Nazi movement had fulfilled the political task of reinvigorating nationalistic feelings that, in a political coalition, the conservatives
could use for their own brand of nationalistic and imperialis-
tic ideas. Young military officers looked gleefully upon the
Blackshirts and Brownshirts as raw material for an army of
the future. By helping Hitler into the saddle the right-wing
parties hoped to reverse the constitutional and social trend of
the Weimar Republic, which tended toward the practical cooperation of capital and labor and the extension of social security and welfare for the people. Conservatives believed that
they could wear down Hitler's authority by shifting governmental responsibility to him during the depth of the depression. Thus, the reactionary figures counted on shaping Hitler
into a compliant, compromising member of a permanent,
strong, right-wing coalition.

In spite of the clear prediction of Hitler and his guards, the
former so-called elite of German society did not foresee that
Hitler could uncompromisingly fulfill his plans and program.
They did not even realize that Hitler would dissolve or coordi-
nate politically (*gleichschalten*) the former groupings and associations of German society to destroy the basis of power of
the conservative, bourgeois groups together with that of the
workers. As a matter of fact, Hitler at once assumed full totalitarian power and gave the control of the government and of
all economic and political groupings to his own party. Consistent with his proven methods of organization, the party mem-

bers had to propagandize and control the masses. From the day he took office, Hitler used the same organizational set-up with which he had once built up the Nazi movement in order to control, to propagandize, and thus, to conquer the German people, breaking down, as far as possible, the differentiated structure of German society. Thus, it should be clear that Hitler's coming into governmental office had nothing directly to do with his ideas. But after he had got hold of the reins of power his policies were based on his ideas, the strict organization, and the revolutionary mass.

By this heterogeneous alliance with Hitler, the former Wilhelmian ruling strata destroyed the very foundation not only of their political but also, to a large degree, of their social and economic positions. They became the vassals of a new order that was no less alien to their tradition than it was to the mode of life of the average farmer and worker. Seldom in history have the elite of a people committed such a suicidal blunder as did the German conservatives and bourgeoisie.

Yet, not many people outside Germany had any clearer understanding of Hitler's revolutionary force. It is a slight excuse that essential words that Hitler and his fanatics spoke and wrote about "anti-capitalism" and "annihilation of world finance," about "unification of the Germans" all over the world, about "vital space" and "conquest of the East" (*Drang nach Osten*), about "racial superiority" of the German people and "persecution of the Jews," and last, about the "fight for world hegemony" could hardly be translated and, therefore, could not really be apprehended in any other language. Split into pros and cons, both fascinated and deeply shocked, the people of the earth have seen their world undergo a thorough change. At the same time, they have hardly been able to understand the aims and bounds of the man Hitler and of his system as these are laid down in *Mein Kampf*.

For years the world has been longing for a breathing spell to collect its thoughts in order to systematically understand the intention of a man who, with a strong hand, interfered with history or, at least, with the evolutionary process of the postwar period. This breathing spell, however, has never come. All that was left, even for those able to make the intellectual effort of finding out whether there is a method in this madness, was to read the hundreds of puzzling books about Hitler and about national socialism. But there is no thorough analysis of Hitler's own writings and of those of his nearest adherents that can make them understand the inner driving force that will enable them to grasp the why of his domestic and foreign policy after his rise to power. Hitler and the Nazis make such an understanding difficult since, in the guise of unbelievable frankness, they try to hide their actions under a smokescreen of denials. They like to take full cover under a camouflage of sympathizers such as Hjalmar Schacht or Carl Gördeler, who still believe in reforming Hitler and in purging the radical Nazis.

Hitler never changed his real and total goals, methods, and techniques. During the thirties Hitler in his speeches and his Nazi friends in their commentaries offered, more or less, tactics: now disguising the ends before the foreigners at home and abroad, now emphasizing them in order to continue revolutionary action. Today it is obvious that the foreign policy of Hitler, in spite of his outspoken sense of the concrete in a political situation, tended to be in accordance with his ideals of foreign policy, which were derived from his ideology. It was the inescapable force of his ideas that shaped Hitler's single-minded policy leading to war.

* * *

From the beginning it was decisive for Hitler's success that his ideas met a peculiar sociological constellation in Germany. In it were merged the social interests of waning or threatened class positions (*i.e.*, officers and middle classes); economic interests (*i.e.*, the farmers and unemployed); and not least, the vague groping, especially of the German youth, for goals in life that transcended "material" interests. Hitler knew intuitively that ideas as such cannot develop in the socioeconomic setting and take hold of specific groups, no matter how susceptible these groups, unless an organized relation is established between the ideas and the masses. Moreover, the envisaged rapport with the masses was contingent on a specific quality of propaganda, namely one that derived its keynotes from the final and unalterable ideas. By this threefold interplay—idea, organization, and the specific nature of the propaganda—Hitler put his system into action.

Later, his success and this continuous awareness of his success finally surrounded Hitler with the halo of invincibility and constantly reenforced the strength of the movement. To be specific, Hitler's success in the battle against unemployment and, above all, the reconstruction of the army and his formal tearing up of the Versailles treaties secured him his following. Even intellectuals who still denied Hitler's assumptions wavered because of the results of Hitler's systematic and efficient procedure. For example, a host of opportunists tried to take material advantage shortly before and after Hitler came to power by loudly proclaiming Hitler's cause as their own, intoxicating themselves on Hitler's ideas with their own applause.

Indeed, the number of close adherents selected from this inflated mass-reservoir grew. It dominated every phase of the life of a German from the Gestapo to the SS Guards and block wardens. Propaganda and adult education tended to become nearly identical. Even the teachings of the natural sciences were used for political suffocation. Goebbels' hammering upset the minds even of the older people and shifted their former concepts of freedom and democracy to freedom for the German people and to mass acclamations, which were still called elections and plebiscites. The education of the younger generation in the new doctrine became a crucial endeavour. In a monopolistic way the Nazis implanted the new values of the warrior nation, grouping the youth and drawing them together in an interlocking network of training institutions from the Hitler Youth to the Labor Service.

Yet, there still remained many millions of Germans bewildered, disturbed, and passive. At least a thousand times, particularly in Anglo-Saxon countries, the questions were posed: Why did not the suppressed democratic ideals in the thin intellectual stratum and, above all, in the bulk of the democratically inculcated workers stimulate fervent reaction at least against concentration camps and arbitrary party rule? Why did this peace-, justice-, and truth-loving part of the people not object to, and thereby prevent, the more or less secret preparations for war? Democratic ideals, as long as they are not contested for, have not by nature the glamour and aggressive character of "doctrines." Concepts of justice and of the recognition of the rights of other human beings are rather a plain way of life. Extraneous factors nipped any such incipient countermovement in the bud.

In a democratic world it seems difficult to understand that a political machine can exercise absolute control over communication. As long as there were no media and no tools, such as free press, free meetings, free speech, and free associations, there was not the slightest possibility for any realization of resistance. There were many brave, unknown fighters among all strata of society who sacrificed their own lives and happiness and that of their families. But this resistance remained an individual or, at the most, local opposition. On the other hand, the totalitarian power of Hitler never succeeded in completely aligning the military sector with the Nazi party. The strict Prussian tradition and ethics were inalienable parts of the army. Also, the old governmental bureaucracy and the private business bureaucracy in the trusts, cartels, and trade associations still existed and often succeeded in smoothing down and even in preventing the cruel and inequitable methods of Nazi administration. The Nazis, however, succeeded in localizing such clashes so that political issues were avoided. In spite of the brave stand of pastors and priests, conflict with the churches remained isolated and restricted to questions of religious independence and autonomy of the churches. Since 1935, as we can see from the Nazi labor press, Goebbels and, more so, Robert Ley, the Labor Front leader, did not need to exert themselves too much to propagandize Hitler's "socialism." From then on labor propaganda restricted itself to feeding the working people with their own specific problems.

Essentially, the totalitarian system did not require the 100 percent conviction of the people as a whole. As long as there were two or three million active adherents organized into well-disciplined groups, the total control of the people was assured. The Nazis did not even need to convert the majority of the population to their ideas as long as there was a responsive process between the upper stratum of the Nazis and this mass of convinced followers who communicated their ideas in continuous action by propaganda and mass show. What mattered, indeed, for the Nazis was a great compact mass of followers but only in conjunction with the quality of the contact: *i.e.,* the vitality of the intercourse between them and the guiding elite. The propaganda continuously referred any given situation to the "final ideas" in a way that the masses felt was convincing and conclusive. The permanent, revolutionary spirit of the Nazi movement could only be sustained through the continuous activization of its doctrines. As Hitler marched into Poland, his final war aims had become an integral part in the psychic makeup of a compact mass of fighters within the army as well as on the home front. In this manner Hitler was able to control Germany and bend it to his will.

2 ⚑ Hitler's Lebensraum: Reason and Character

I

In lengthily reasoned deliberations Hitler tried to sell his expansionist program to his adherents. He did not need to offer detailed proof for the right to unify all Germans in one Reich. The German nation established a right to be unified on the basis of the principle of self-determination of nations, a principle generally recognized, but not observed in the case of Germany in the years after the first world war. Hitler realized that he had to offer impressive reasons to the Germans to inspire them with his plan to conquer the lebensraum since it implied great renunciations in the petty comforts of the Germans.[1] He cited overpopulation as the main cause of German dependency on other countries, which would result in economic crises and starvation. He identified four roads, crucial to Germany's future, by which to overcome its far-reaching consequences. In doing so he dwelled with great satisfaction on the utterly mistaken foreign policy of the kaiser, and he repudiated as decadent the alternative manner of handling the problem by birth control measures—all this in order to force his reader to follow him on the road to the only possible solution—the lebensraum.

---

1. The term *lebensraum* has been incorporated into the English language. The definition given in the "New Words" section of the 1942 edition of *Webster's Collegiate Dictionary* reads, in part, "territory, especially additional territory, essential to a nation's expansion, as for trade or emigration."

What is the expansionist scheme which Adolf Hitler designed long before he came to power? The expansionist scheme may be described as the step-by-step widening of Germany's orbit and power in the form of four concentric circles. The innermost circle represents the Reich within the boundaries of Versailles, which distends into the next circle by absorbing the Germans living abroad. In the third state, the lebensraum is conquered to be settled in the future by racial Germans. The lebensraum, in turn, is the precondition for expansion into the next circle, namely, European hegemony. Finally, the hegemony is to be extended over the entire globe.

* * *

The first two phases of the Führer's expansionist program—the integration of all Germans into one Reich and the conquest of lebensraum—had already been sketchily outlined in the party program of 1920. Point one of the program reads as follows: "We demand, on the basis of the right of national self-determination, the union of all Germans to form one Great Germany." In point three of the program, the lebensraum is indicated in the following form: "We demand territory and soil (colonies) for the nourishment of our people and for settling our surplus population."[2] Hitler, in Mein Kampf, placed the incorporation of the German abroad into the German body politic ahead of the conquest of new, non-German territory.[3]

2. Gottfried Feder, Das Programm der N.S.D.A.P. und seine Weltanschaulichen Grundgedanken (Munich: Nationalsozialistische Bibliothek, Heft 1, 1933), 19. For the complete text of the program of Hitler's National Socialist German Labor party, see Appendix A. The term colonies was used by Hitler and his party indiscriminately for two different concepts: colonization of adjoining lands and of overseas territories. The party program left open whether the term colonies meant demands for settlement in Europe or overseas. Hitler used the term colonies in the twofold concept, too; however, he decided clearly, as we shall see later, in favor of colonization in Europe.

3. Colonization (Kolonialpolitische Tatigkeit) obviously means here colonization of land in Europe now settled by non-German peoples.

❘Hitler agreed that "Common blood belongs in a common Reich. As long as the German nation is unable even to band together its own children in one common State, it has no moral right to think of colonization as one of its political aims. Only when the boundaries of the Reich include even the last German, only when it is no longer possible to assure him of daily bread inside them, does there arise, out of the distress of the nation, the moral right to acquire foreign soil and territory. The sword is then the plow, and from the tears of war there grows the daily bread for generations to come."[4] The solution of the irredentist program, comprising the return of "approximately more than 7,000,000" Germans who "languish under alien rule" (917), presupposes the restoration of the Reich as a strong European power.[5]

"What must guide us constantly today," Hitler declared, "is the fundamental insight that the regaining of lost imperial territories is primarily a question of regaining the political independence and power of the motherland" (917).[6] He stated that such a task cannot be solved by a parliament, by prayers, or by negotiations before the League of Nations, but only by blood and iron. "One must be quite clear about the fact that the regaining of the lost regions will not come about through solemn appeals to the dear Lord or through pious hopes in a League of Nations, but only by force of arms," he wrote, and "today I am guided by the sober knowledge that one does not regain lost territories by means of the glibness of tongue of sharp parliamentarian gabblers, but that one must regain them by means of a sharp sword, that is, through a bloody

4. Adolf Hitler, *Mein Kampf* (New York: Reynal and Hitchcock, 1939), 3, hereinafter cited in the text by page number only.

5. Hitler did not include the Austrian population in this figure.

6. The context suggests that the "lost imperial territories" were not restricted to the provinces severed from the Reich by the Treaty of Versailles. They obviously included territory settled by Germany outside the old imperial Germany, such as Sudeten Germany.

struggle" (912, 916). Again, he wrote, "For oppressed countries will not be brought back into the bosom of a common Reich by means of fiery protests, but by a mighty sword. To forge this sword is the task of the domestic political leadership of a people; to guard the work of forging and to seek comrades in arms is the task of the foreign-policy leadership" (891).

*   *   *

Hitler justified his claim to lebensraum, the acquisition of non-German territory, on the ground that Germany belonged to the "have-not" nations and was overpopulated. In support of Germany's overpopulation, he cited the annual increase of almost 900,000 Germans, prior to 1914.[7] "The difficulty of feeding this army of new citizens," he suggested, "would become greater with every year, and was bound some day to end in a catastrophe, provided ways and means were not found to avert this impending danger of hunger-pauperization in time" (168).

Hitler's overpopulation concept differed strikingly from those developed by generally acknowledged population theoreticians. These consider a country as overpopulated only if it is unable to secure a livelihood for its growing population. It is entirely irrelevant what proportion of foodstuffs or other like necessities is produced within the country or has to be imported from other nations. Under the conditions of international division of labor, every industrial country is obliged to import part of the necessary foodstuffs and vital supplies from other parts of the world by offering its own labor in the form of manufactured products in exchange.

7. As a matter of fact, in the postwar years 1920–1925 (just before Hitler published *Mein Kampf*), the average annual population increase had already dropped to 564,000. We do not know whether Hitler deliberately neglected these vital statistics of the postwar years or whether he had in the back of his mind measures to increase the birth rate and annual rate of growth of the population.

In contrast, Hitler refused to recognize the liberal scheme of world economy against which he postulated "national self-sufficiency." For him, the quantity of food produced within the country provided the only criterion of overpopulation. The idea that Hitler had at the back of his mind when he painted this strange apocalyptic picture of starvation and poverty was the postulate of a self-sufficient Germany that did not exchange industrial products against foodstuffs on the world market. Under his assumption, then, Germany was of course already "overpopulated" under the kaiser, and even a sizable drop in the birth rate would still leave her "overpopulated."

Hitler took great pains to discuss with his followers the ways and means to overcome the perceived dangerous consequences of overpopulation pressure. He pointed to four alternative ways to "avoid such a terrible future." First, one might resort to birth control. But this, he believed, would result in suicide and biological degeneration of the German race, because once the number of births was reduced, one would try to save at any cost even "the weakest and the sickest." He admitted that

> Nature herself, in times of great distress or bad climatic conditions, or where the yields of the soil are poor, steps in by restricting the population of certain countries or races; this, however, is a method that is as wise as it is ruthless. She does not restrict the procreative faculty as such, but the conservation of the propagated, by subjecting them to such severe trials and deprivations that all less strong and healthy are forced to return to the bosom of the eternally Unknown. . . .
>
> But [he insisted] it is different if man decides to carry out the restriction of his numbers. . . .
>
> . . . This correction of the divine will seems to him to be as wise as it is human, and he is glad that he has outwitted Nature once more in such a matter, and that he even has given proof of her shortcomings. But, of course, the Lord's dear little monkey does

not at all like to see or to hear that in reality, although the number had certainly been restricted, the value of the individual has been diminished.

Because, once propagation as such has been limited and the number of births reduced, the natural struggle for existence, that allows only the very strongest and healthiest to survive, is replaced by the natural urge to 'save' at any price also the weakest and even sickest, thus planting the germ for a succession that is bound to become more and more miserable the longer this derision of Nature and of her will is continued.

But the result will be that one day existence in this world will be denied such a people. . . .

He who, therefore, would secure the German people's existence by way of a self-restriction of its increase robs it of its future. (169–71)

The second possibility that Hitler imagined was domestic colonization. But Hitler contended that domestic colonization should serve only to check social abuses and to withdraw the soil from economic speculation. Resettlement of German farmers upon the land within the boundaries of the Reich could not solve the basic overpopulation problem. He wrote, "It cannot be emphasized sharply enough that all German domestic colonization has to serve, primarily, only to abolish social abuses, but above all to withdraw the soil from general speculation, and that it can never suffice to secure the future of the nation without new land and soil" (176). Hitler arrived at this judgment on the basis of the assumption that there is a definite limit to the productivity of the German soil whereas the number of people and their demands for food outstrip this productivity.

Therefore [he argued], one could be able to balance the increase of the German people by the increased yield of our soil for some time, without having to think immediately of hunger. But this is confronted by the fact that, generally, the demands upon life increase faster than the number of the population. . . . at least part of the surplus yield of the soil is used to satisfy the increased demands of men. But even with greatest economy on the one hand, and with the utmost industry on the other, here, also, though postponed for some time, a limit will become apparent one day, prescribed by the soil itself. Famine will return from time to time in periods of poor harvests, etc. (172–73)

Thus, even a sacrifice in the standard of living would not, he believed, in the long run suffice to ward off the dire day when the ratio of the yield of the soil to the population would have deteriorated to such a degree that the specter of famine would become a reality. "This will occur," he predicted, "more and more often with the increasing number of the population, and finally will fail to appear only at such rare times when years of plenty will have filled the granaries. But finally the time comes when it will no longer be possible to satisfy the needs, and famine will have become the eternal companion of such a people" (173).

The third and, to Hitler's mind, the most desirable solution would be for Germany to seize new soil for the settlement of the surplus population "and thus conserve the nation further on the basis of self-sustainment" (178). This additional soil must be in Europe, not overseas. He insisted that "a sound territorial policy was to be found in the acquisition of new soil in Europe proper. Colonies cannot serve this purpose, since they do not appear suitable for settlement with Europeans on a large scale. But in the nineteenth century it was no longer possible to gain such colonial territories in a peaceful way. Such a colonial policy could only have been carried out by means of a hard struggle which would have been fought out more suitably, not for territories outside Europe, but rather for land in the home continent itself" (181).

Adolf Hitler had Russia's soil in mind. He argued that imperial Germany should have resumed the ancient *Drang nach*

Osten of the medieval Teutonic knights. "If one wanted land and soil in Europe," Hitler declared, "then by and large this could only have been done at Russia's expense, and then the new Reich would again have to start marching along the road of the knights of the orders of former times to give, with the help of the German sword, the soil to the plow and the daily bread to the nation"(182–83). Only by war could such a goal be reached. Hitler did not flinch at such a choice. He wrote, "One had to make it clear to oneself that this goal could be reached only through fighting, and quietly to face the passage at arms. . . . Our right to do this would not have been less than that of our forefathers. None of our pacifists refuses to eat the bread of the East, although the first plow was once called 'sword'" (182–83).

To achieve this end, Hitler argued, the kaiser's Germany should have won the friendship of England.

> For such a policy, however, there was only one single ally in Europe: England.
> With England alone, one's back being covered, could one begin the new Germanic invasion. . . .
> To gain England's favor, no sacrifice should have been too great. Then one would have had to renounce colonies and sea power, but to spare British industry our competition.
> Only an unconditionally clear attitude could lead to such a goal: renouncing world trade and colonies; renouncing a German war fleet. Concentration of the State's entire means of power in the land army.
> The result would certainly have been a momentary restriction, but a great and powerful future. (183–84)

Hitler admitted that this idea had developed in his mind as far back as his painting days.

> I confess openly that in pre-War times I already held it better had Germany, at the sacrifice of the senseless colonial policy and at the sacrifice of the merchant and naval fleet, stood in alliance with England against Russia, and thus switched from the feeble

world-wide policy to a determined European policy of continental territorial acquisition.

I do not forget the constant impudent threat which the then pan-Slav Russia dared level against Germany; I do not forget the constant practice mobilizations whose sole point was to offend Germany; I cannot forget the attitude of Russian public opinion which, even before the War, outdid itself in hateful sallies against our nation and Reich, cannot forget the influential Russian press which always was more enthusiastic for France than for us. (962)

Hitler conceded that prior to World War I the opposite policy, namely, world trade, colonialism, and navalism, with Russia's backing against England, might have constituted a solution worth considering, although, for him, less desirable by far than territorial expansion in the east of Europe. But he believed such a choice was no longer desirable. "Today relations are different." Hitler affirmed, "If, before the War, one could have gone with Russia at the cost of throttling every last feeling, this is today no longer possible (962).

Looking back to the days prior to 1914, Hitler stated,

If Germany, nevertheless, chose this way, then one had at least to recognize clearly that this development also would some day end in fighting. Only children could believe that, through friendly and civilized behavior and continued emphasis on a friendly disposition, could they gather their 'bananas' in a 'peaceful competition of nations,' as one so nicely and unctuously chattered, without ever being forced to take up arms.

No, if we went this way, then England would some day become our enemy. It was more absurd to get indignant at this, but it was in keeping with our own harmlessness that England took the liberty of some day meeting our peaceful activity with the brutality of the violent egoist.

We, I regret to say, would never have done this. (187–88)

The Hohenzellern Reich, Hitler asserted, did not travel the road toward the East nor did it face the consequences of the less desirable opposite course of world trade and colonies, because it had lost the heroic and belligerent spirit. The preservation of world peace, Hitler charged, had become an obsession. The welfare of the world was valued more highly than the national interest.

> One feared nothing more than a fight [he insisted], so that finally in the least favorable hour one was nevertheless forced into it.
>
> One tried to escape Fate and was overtaken by it. One dreamed of the preservation of world peace and landed in the World War.
>
> For this was the most important reason why one never considered this third way of the formation of a German future. One knew that the acquisition of new soil was to be attained only in the East, and one saw the necessary fight, and yet one wanted peace at any price; for the watchword of German foreign politics had long ceased to be, preservation of the German nation by all means, but rather, preservation of the world peace by all available means. (186–87)

It was self-deception, Hitler argued, to believe in the possibility of a peaceful solution of Germany's overpopulation problem. With the "peaceful economic" conquest of the world one had a formula which was supposed to break the neck of the former policy of force once and for all. But this "talk of the 'peaceful economic conquest' of the world was certainly," for Hitler, "the greatest folly that was ever made the leading principle of a State policy" (188).

Hitler's criticism was not based on the fact that this policy led to war. War, he thought, was inevitable. But Germany had drifted into a war, the avoidance of which was the very purpose of her pacifist policy. This specific and halfhearted policy left Germany without the backing of a strong ally—a situation that had to end in final defeat by a world united against Germany.

The fourth road, that of overseas colonization, world trade, and navalism, was the road along which imperial Germany had traveled. "Of the four roads to a future preservation of our nationality and its maintenance," Hitler declared, "the fourth and least favorable was chosen. In place of a healthy European land policy, a colonial and trade policy was adopted. This was particularly erroneous as it was then imagined that thereby a settlement by arms could be evaded" (891–92). Furthermore, he charged that world trade as a basis of national life had an unwholesome effect on the social body of Germany. "The first consequence of gravest importance," he insisted, "was the weakening of the peasant class. In the same measure in which the latter class diminished, the mass of the proletariat of the great cities grew more and more, till finally the balance was lost entirely. Now the sharp contrast between poor and rich became really apparent" (315–16).

Hitler argued that wealth on one side and distress and frequent unemployment on the other led to discontent and class struggle. "Superabundance and misery now lived so close together that the consequences of this could be and were bound to be necessarily very dreary. Distress and frequent unemployment began to play their game with people and left discontent and embitterment as a memory behind them. The consequence of this seemed to be the political class split" (316).

Hitler condemned this class split because it rent the nation in two; it was the very opposite of his ideal of national unity and coherence. An even worse consequence of such one-sided industrialization, according to Hitler, was the corruption of the national spirit and of the heroic virtues by capitalistic money ideology. "Worse than this were other consequential symptoms which the economization of the nation brought with it," he wrote. "In the measure in which business rose to become the determining master of the State, money became the god whom now everybody had to serve and to worship. . . . A truly evil degeneration thus set in, especially evil for the reason that this took place at a time when the nation, more than ever, would probably need the highest heroic conviction at a threatening critical hour" (316–17). Adolf Hitler reproached the kaiser and even Bismarck for having furthered such spiritual decay.

The theory that underlay Hitler's reasoning represents a recrudescence of the Malthusian population law, with the added promise, however, that self-sufficiency in foodstuffs must be guaranteed within the bounds of the nation. But, while Malthus proposed "moral restraint" as the solution of overpopulation, Hitler rejected any artificial check on population because it would endanger the future of the German race. The only solution for Hitler was seizure of new land. More than that, he considered it a national duty even to counteract the trend towards population decrease and thus to provide reason for still further expansion. (His population policy after 1933 aimed at encouraging marriages and illegitimate births and suppressing birth control devices and institutions.)

The Malthusian laws—valid for an economy where production follows traditional patterns and where the increase of population is the only dynamic factor—were no longer in operation under the current international division of labor and in the application of modern science and technology. Nevertheless, Malthusianism celebrated its resurrection in *Mein Kampf* and thus provided the leitmotif for conquest which had now become a fearful reality. Hitler's success in employing this argument testifies to his bizarre dialectical mastery. He simply started out with the (tacit) dogmatic postulate of a self-sufficient Germany, a Germany closely resembling the utopian closed commercial state whose prophet was the German philosopher Fichte (1762–1814). Like Fichte, Hitler considered economic independence a natural corollary of any healthy national state. In the magic mirror of such self-sufficiency, Germany suddenly appeared overpopulated, as would indeed any country that, even under modern agricultural methods, fed part of its population by importing foodstuffs. The tortuous workings of Hitler's mind are revealed by the manner in which he proposed a seemingly practical cure for an overpopulation that was arbitrarily called into existence on the basis of a political assumption regarding Germany as an independent and isolated economic unit in the world.

II

According to Hitler the future lebensraum in the East had to be conquered. This contiguous territory had to be large enough so that 250 million Germans could live on the continent a hundred years hence. Hitler had a definite conception of the socioeconomic structure of this new and enlarged Germany. A balance between industry and agriculture provided the indispensable basis for a healthy and strong nation imbued with a new heroic spirit. This was necessary for Germany to obtain world power status at a time when the world was divided among empires like England and France, and continental nations like the United States. Not only was population pressure as "push" an argument for conquest of lebensraum, but the ideal socioeconomic structure in the lebensraum was, as "pull," an even more powerful reason for exacting heavy, though temporary, sacrifices to secure it. Hitler adduced the overpopulation argument as a necessity for expansion. He envisioned the lebensraum as the condition for a pure race, a healthy *Volk* (people) and a united nation.

With the expansion of Germany into new lebensraum an "autarkic Reich" was to be established. Although Hitler did not use the word *autarky*, this term best characterizes the peculiar socioeconomic order that he envisaged for his new lebensraum. The term *autarky* is generally employed by "liberal" economists who see the world only in economic terms to signify a situation of national economic self-sufficiency or a policy leading in this direction of establishing independence of imports from foreign countries.[8] But Hitler's concept of autarky is more specific and more inclusive. Hitler's autarky is of a threefold nature. It is conceived of, first, as independence in foodstuffs, second, as equilibrium between agriculture and industry, and third, in the sense of financial independence. While the first and the third of these characteristics make up what is usually and generally understood by self-sufficiency, the second deviates essentially from the common conception. It is an autarky built upon the preconceived idea that industry and agriculture should balance and complement each other without resort to foreign markets since the lack of such a balance, expressed in overindustrialization, in Hitler's opinion, was the root cause of the social ills that jeopardized the internal cohesion of the nation. Thus, the socioeconomic order was, for Hitler, the *sine qua non* of any healthy and really independent state. If autarky was the necessary order of a healthy state and could only be realized within lebensraum, it followed that the demand for autarky was, at the same time, another strong argument for the conquest of lebensraum.

The intertwining of two aspects, self-sufficiency in foodstuffs and an equilibrium between industry and agriculture is clearly indicated in the following statement by Hitler:

> The very possibility of preserving a healthy peasant class as the basis of the entire nation can never be sufficiently valued. To a great extent many of our present sufferings are only the consequences of the unhealthy proportion between town and country population. A solid stock of small and medium peasants was at all times the best protection against social ills as we have them today. This is also the only solution that allows a nation to find its daily bread in the inner circle of its domestic economy. Industry and trade step back from their unwholesome leading positions into the general frame of a national economy of balanced demand and sup-

8. The term *autarky* has also been incorporated into the English language. The "New Words" section of the 1942 edition of *Webster's Collegiate Dictionary* defines *autarky* as "National economic self-sufficiency; a policy of establishing independence of imports from other countries."

ply. Both are then no longer the basis of a nation's subsistence, but a means to it. Inasmuch as now they have a balance between their supply and demand in all fields, they make the entire support of the nation independent of foreign countries, thus helping to secure the liberty of the state and the independence of the nation, especially in times of distress. (178–79)

In order to correct this prevailing imbalance, Hitler believed that no sacrifice of blood was too great, and that the newly acquired territory should be colonized with German peasants. He wrote, "The soil and territory on which a race of German peasants will some day be able to beget sons sanction the investment of the sons of today, and will some day acquit the responsible statesmen of blood and guilt and national sacrifice, even though they be persecuted by their contemporaries" (948). His interest was centered on the insurance of self-sufficiency in food supply and a healthy peasant class, which were for him the criteria of a healthy state. In his words, "Moreover, only that relationship can ever be regarded as healthy which assures the nourishment of a people from its own soil and territory. Every other situation, though it may last centuries and even millennia, is nevertheless unhealthy, and will sooner or later lead to the injuring if not the destruction of the people concerned" (935).

Hitler stated, "Today we are eighty million Germans in Europe! That foreign policy will be acknowledged as correct only if, a bare century from now, two hundred and fifty million Germans are living on this continent, and then not squeezed together as factory coolies for the rest of the world, but: as peasants and workers mutually guaranteeing each other's life by their productivity" (979). Hitler's ideal Germany was one in which the German worker would produce industrial goods for the increasing number of German peasants and in turn be fed by these peasants; national production and consumption would be brought into a dynamic balance.

Whether, in the light of the needs of industry, such an empire could be truly self-sufficient evidently did not interest Hitler who followed visionary perspectives alone, not factual economic circumstances—thus subduing industrial economic trends to the arbitrary path set by his philosophy.

* * *

Hitler gave a third reason for autarky, namely, independence from international finance capital. Hitler stressed that Germany's economic regime was already under the thumb of international finance capital in the days of the kaiser's empire. "The internationalization," he wrote, "of German economic life had been introduced even before the War by the roundabout way of stock issues" (320). He believed that he had discovered the alliance between international capitalism and international Marxism. "Indeed," Hitler declared, "one part of German industry still tried to guard itself with determination against this fate; but then, in turn, it fell victim to the combined attack of greedy capital fighting this battle especially with the aid of its faithful comrade, the Marxist movement" (320–21). He asserted that under the Weimar Republic this process was accelerated. "While I am writing this," said Hitler, "the general attack against the German State Railways, which is now handed over to international capital, has finally been successful" (321). Therefore, "the fight against international finance and loan capital has become the most important point in the program of the German nation's fight for its independence and freedom" (288).

* * *

Hitler demanded that territory newly acquired by National Socialist Germany be settled with German peasants. He omitted in this context the fate of the non-German population of these lands. "What in history," he asserted, "has been profitably Ger-

manized was the soil which our forefathers acquired through
the sword and settled with German peasants" (591). And
"a *Germanization* can only be carried out with the *soil* and
never with *men*" (588).

Hitler decried the pan-German movement in Austria that,
before the war of 1914, tried to Germanize the Slavs in the
Austro-Hungarian monarchy by imposing the German language upon them. He wrote:

> But it is a hardly conceivable mistake in thinking to believe
> that, let us say, a negro or a Chinese would become a German be-
> cause he learns German and is prepared to speak the German lan-
> guage in the future and perhaps to give his vote to a German
> political party. It never became clear to our bourgeois national
> world that any Germanization of this kind is in reality a de-
> Germanization. . . .
>
> But not only in Austria, also in Germany herself the so-called
> national circles were and are motivated by similar wrong trends of
> thought. The Polish policy in the sense of a Germanization of the
> East, demanded by so many, rooted unfortunately almost always
> in the same wrong conclusion. Here too one believed that one
> could bring about a Germanization of the Polish element by a
> purely linguistic integration into the German nationality. Here
> too the result would have been an unfortunate one: people of an
> alien race, expressing its alien thoughts in the German language,
> compromising the height and the dignity of our own nationality
> by its own inferiority. (588, 590)

The German people was, for Hitler, the potential German
race. It was not the unity of language that constituted a nation
but its racial unity. In his words, "nationality, or rather the
race, is not rooted in the language but in the blood" (589).

Hitler violently denounced the imposition of the German
language upon what he considered inferior races. He called
such a process de-Germanization, because he believed that
such an "enforced outward acceptance of the German language" jeopardized the racial purity of the German nation and

if carried on over a long period and on a huge scale would finally lead to the loss of the nation's racial identity. A mechanical expansion of Germany's linguistic frontiers "would mean the beginning of a hybridization and with this, in our case, not a Germanization but a destruction of the Germanic element. In history it happens only too frequently that the outward means of power of a conquering people succeeds in forcing their language upon the oppressed, but that after a thousand years their language is spoken by a different people and the conquerors thus become actually the vanquished" (589).

Hitler restricted himself in *Mein Kampf* to a few general suggestions relating to the territorial expanse of the lebensraum and its prospective place on the map, and he carefully avoided committing himself to any definite geographical boundaries. The size of the lebensraum was to be broadly determined by three considerations: autarky, strategy, and prestige. First, the lebensraum must be large enough to insure Hitler's ideal of autarky. He wrote, "The foreign policy of a folkish State is charged with guaranteeing the existence on this planet of the race embraced by the State, by establishing between the number and growth of the population, on the one hand, and the size and value of the soil and territory, on the other hand, a viable, natural relationship" (935). This statement must be understood under its long-term aspect: it concerned not only the present generation, but the future generations as well. "Never," he argued, "regard the Reich as secure while it is unable to give every national offshoot for centuries his own bit of soil and territory" (964). If we recall Hitler's demographic "forecast" of 250 million Germans within a century's time, it may readily be conjectured how much land would be required for the German population in four or five hundred years.

Second, the lebensraum had to be large enough to afford military protection.

> The necessary extent of the domain to be occupied [Hitler asserted] cannot be judged exclusively by contemporary requirements, nor even by the quantity of the produce of the soil compared to the population. . . . the area of a State has also another, military-political significance than as a direct source of nourishment of a people. When a people has secured its nourishment for itself by virtue of the extent of its soil and territory, it is nevertheless necessary to think also of securing the territory in hand. This depends on the State's general power-political force and strength which is to no small extent conditioned by geo-military considerations. (935–36)

He offered the same strategical considerations in another passage: "The greater the amount of room a people has at its disposal, the greater is also its natural protection; because military victories over nations crowded in small territories have always been reached more quickly and more easily . . . than in the cases of States which are territorially greater in size. The size of the State territory, therefore, gives a certain protection against frivolous attacks, as success may be gained only after long and severe fighting and, therefore, the risk of an impertinent surprise attack, except for quite unusual reasons, will appear too great" (177).

Third, the lebensraum must be large enough to command prestige and renown for Germany in the eyes of the world. To Hitler large territory is a matter of national prestige—an attribute of world power and importance. He declared, "To be a world power . . . it requires that size which nowadays gives its necessary importance to such a power" (950). "In an epoch when the earth is gradually being divided among States, some of which encompass almost whole continents, one cannot speak of a structure as a world power the political mother country of which is limited to the ridiculous area of barely five hundred thousand square kilometers" (936). Beyond this Hitler did not specify except that it must be a contiguous territory located in Europe, more specifically, in the east.

According to Hitler, the lebensraum must constitute a coherent large area in Europe and must not extend to some overseas colonial land, first of all, because a nation based on contiguous territory had better chances of survival. Hitler praised the territorial structure of the United States as the ideal to which the colonial empires of Europe were politically inferior. "Many European States today," he affirmed, "are comparable to pyramids standing on their points. Their European territory is ridiculously small as compared with their burden of colonies, foreign trade, etc. One may say, the point is in Europe, the base in the whole world; in comparison with the American Union, which still has its bases in its own continent and touches the remaining part of the world only with its points. From this results, however, the unheard-of internal strength of this State and the weakness of most of the European colonial powers" (180). Applying this doctrine to Germany, Hitler insisted that he would "find this question's solution not in colonial acquisitions, but exclusively in the winning of land for settlement which increases the area of the motherland itself, and thereby not only keeps the new settlers in the most intimate community with the land of origin, but insures to the total area those advantages deriving from its united magnitude" (950).

A further argument that he made against the acquisition of colonial possessions overseas has already been discussed. Colonies suited for settlement by Europeans, Hitler argued, were already taken by other powers. The remaining space overseas was not fit for German peasants. But such colonies suitable for German settlement could be wrested from their

owners only by a war effort that it would be more expedient to
devote to the conquest of soil on the home continent itself.
Furthermore, he believed that only a large Germany in Europe
was a sufficient guarantee for Germany's hegemony in Europe.
Hitler clearly indicated that the general direction of expansion within Europe was to be eastward. This meant *"Drang
nach Osten"* was the slogan. He wrote, "But if we talk about
new soil and territory in Europe today, we can think primarily
only of Russia and its vassal border states" (950–51). "We National Socialists consciously draw a line through the foreign-
policy trend of our pre-War period. We take up at the halting
place of six hundred years ago. We terminate the endless German drive to the south and west of Europe, and direct our gaze
towards the lands in the east. We finally terminate the colonial and trade policy of the pre-War period, and proceed to the
territorial policy of the future" (950). The reasons for the east-
erly orientation can be deduced from Hitler's references to the
"wide-open spaces," *i.e.*, the sparsely settled areas in the east,
and from his utter contempt for the Slavs as inferior peoples.

It is frequently assumed that Karl Haushofer, the geopolitician, had participated in Hitler's so-called brain trust when he
wrote *Mein Kampf*. There is no evidence to corroborate or
prove such an assumption. Hitler very likely had known Haushofer's studies, but it is mistaken to believe that Hitler's lebensraum concept is identical with Haushofer's space (*Raum*)
concept of geopolitics. The geopolitical school declared geog-
raphy (topography, climate, material resources) the determining factor in the rise and fall of nations. Geographical factors,
particularly the geographical position of a country, ordained
foreign policy in its decisive features. For Hitler it was not
the physical setting that shaped the destiny of nations, but the
race. Lebensraum for Hitler was decisively bound up with the
racial problem. Haushofer, on the other hand, always em-

ployed the term *Lebensraum* in a purely geographical sense, with complete disregard of race as an influential or determining factor.

Although Hitler may have been influenced by the formal aspects of Haushofer's theory, according to Hitler's formulation of the geographical problems, it was Friedrich Ratzel who had guided his pen. It was only after Hitler's rise to power that the old geopolitician bowed to Hitler's racial doctrines, thereby painfully cramping his own style as a geographical determinist. Haushofer—like many German scholars—was "*gleichschalt*-ed" (coordinated politically and, in this case, intellectually). The Nazis, of course, made good use of Haushofer's Geopolitical Institute as a valuable source of information on the countries to be conquered. That again does not mean that the foreign policy or even the strategy was made in Professor Haushofer's geopolitical laboratory. Haushofer's institute was but one among many academic institutions that the Nazis found useful as ammunition factories for the war of nerves.

3 ⌘ Hitler's Racism and the New World Order

I

According to Hitler the new land (lebensraum) would help to bring about a racially purified, healthy German people united by sound herd instinct. These basic conditions would guarantee German hegemony in Europe and, above all, enable her to follow the call to fulfill her "mission" in the world. Hitler's aspirations were far from being confined to Europe; he meant to achieve German world domination. Such a world mastery by one nation, he argued, would bring peace to this earth. Yet world conquest and world peace were not, for Hitler, ends in themselves. They were means by which to usher in a new epoch of Aryan culture. For the Germans to become masters of the globe and to give a new culture to this earth—these, indeed, were the real war aims of Hitler. These positive war aims fascinated and inspired German soldier-idealists. Many have discussed Hitler's intentions with regard to the new order in Europe; few realize that this "order" was actually the beginning of a worldwide revolution against the prevailing political and cultural world structure.

In the following discussion I use the terms *nation* and *people* interchangeably since, in the English translation of *Mein Kampf* from which I quote, the English equivalent of *Volk* has been rendered indiscriminately by *nation* and *people*; *Volkstum* (actually folkdom) and *Volkskörper* (folkish body) have

53

been translated, respectively, as *nationality* and *national body*. In observing this usage of the translation we were aware that we have done away with the distinction, fairly consistently maintained in the original *Mein Kampf*, between *Volk* (people) and *Nation* (nation). In referring to prenational periods Hitler dealt only with the characteristics and the functional relationship of race, *Volk*, and state; but for modern history he distinguished between nation, *Volk*, race, and state in the following manner: In speaking of a *Volk* living at the present time he thought less of its common political ties, and more of its racial qualities, its common culture and common spirit or soul (*Volksseele*). He gave the concept *Volk* a "folkish" (*i.e.*, romantic) connotation. For Hitler it was the *Volk*— and the *Volk* only—that can possess the herd instinct, that has tradition, language, art, music, "folkways," and mores in common.

In contrast, the modern *nation* meant for Hitler a unit by virtue of a common political history. The nation was expressive of the actual or potential political power of this unit. National consciousness, based on a common political past and common aspirations in the political field, constituted a real nation. The value, the vitality and the strength of the people (*Volk*), Hitler argued, was determined by its racial composition. A nation made up of different peoples, composed of different racial elements, and therefore holding a number of different concepts of life could not endure, unless the core people—the potential master race—with its capacity for organization and its creative gift in the sphere of culture and politics gained the upper hand over the other peoples constituting the nation.

Although race was fundamentally a biological concept for Hitler, it contained, at the same time, an overwhelming historico-metaphysical factor of determinism; the innate qualities of a race determined its political and cultural fate (thus only Aryans were capable of creating culture in this world).

The state arises from conquest. It is a political, protective, and administrative instrument. For Hitler the organic inter-relationship between race, *Volk*, nation, and state meant that if a people were racially uniform, it would possess the herd instinct, which, in the long run, would make for a united nation and national (*i.e.*, power) consciousness. The state was the instrument by which to preserve the race, to foster innate capacities of the people, and to increase the power of the nation. "One day there can exist," Hitler wrote, "a State which represents . . . a folkish organism: *A Germanic State of the German Nation.*"[1]

Race for Hitler, was the alpha and omega of nature and history: "All great questions of the times," he declared, "are questions of the moment, and they represent only consequences of certain causes. Only one of them is of causal importance, that is the question of the racial preservation of the nationality [*Volkstum*]. In the blood alone there rests the strength as well as the weakness of man" (469). Strength and weakness of nations depended upon their racial composition. The purer a nation in its racial make-up, the stronger it would be. National solidarity was a quality inherent in every nation that retained its original racial purity intact. Such a purebred nation possessed as a natural endowment what Hitler called the herd instinct. He wrote, "sure herd instinct . . . guards the nation [*Nation*] against ruin especially in dangerous moments, as with such peoples all the minor internal differences usually disappear immediately and the common enemy is confronted by the closed front of a uniform herd" (598).

What Hitler called herd instinct must not be confounded

1. Adolf Hitler, *Mein Kampf* (New York: Reynal and Hitchcock, 1939), 455, hereinafter cited in the text by page number only.

with race instinct. The herd instinct of a people described a psychological attitude that could be developed only in the case of a complete racial uniformity (accomplished by the purity of the original race or by a thoroughly mixed and, thus, uniform stock) of all the members of a group. Herd instinct was the psychological attitude characteristic of a homogeneous group, which guaranteed its unity. Race instinct was an instinct inherent in the individual members of a race. By virtue of it the individual was able to sense and to guard against foreign blood. According to Hitler a pure race possessed undiluted herd instinct from which it derived its cohesion and power. But such a race was always threatened with contamination since the individual might be forgetful of his race instinct. If there was race defilement, the racial group would lose its homogeneity and therewith its herd instinct. Disunity and inner conflict would accompany this loss. In order to prevent the loss of racial integrity by the individual, so that the purity of the race would not be endangered, Hitler asked for strong laws against actual or attempted race defilement.

Racial uniformity, for Hitler, was obviously indispensable for the unity of a nation. Yet he recognized in history that very often uniformity of race is not a quality possessed by purebred nations alone. It was equally shared by peoples originally composed of different racial stocks but fused together by intermarriage into a new and homogeneous race. Such a uniform mixture, a product of a final blending over a long series of generations, also engendered that "sure herd instinct which is rooted in the unity of the blood" (598).

Nonetheless, such a crossbred nation, he believed, was at a fateful disadvantage in comparison with a pure race. It paid a terrible price for the uniformity of blood and the herd instinct which it did not possess originally, but had acquired by intense hybridization. Hitler argued that the crossbred progeny was invariably inferior to the parent stock. Hence any hybrid race was doomed to cultural inferiority. Hitler referred specifically to Austria. He discussed the Germanization policy of Joseph II, Emperor of Austria in the Age of Enlightenment. Joseph II made the abortive attempt to impose the German language on his subjects, which included Czechs, Poles, and Croats, to consolidate his empire. Herein, Hitler believed, lay the error of Joseph's policy. Hitler wrote, "Its success would probably have been the conservation of the Austrian State, but also the lowering of the racial level of the German nation [*Nation*] brought about by a linguistic community. In the course of the centuries a certain herd instinct would certainly have crystallized itself, but the herd itself would have become inferior. Perhaps a State people would have been born, but a culture people would have lost" (589–90).

Hitler argued that the lowering of the cultural and spiritual standard was not the only punishment meted out by nature for the crime of hybridization. A nation made up of hybrids was also bound to succumb in the struggle for existence against a nation of pure race. Suppose, he suggested, that "in the course of thousands of years" there would be formed

a new mixture in which the original individual elements, in consequence of a thousandfold crossing, are completely mixed and no longer recognizable. Thus a new nationality [*Volkstum*] with a certain herd-like resistibility would have been formed, but compared with the highest race which helped in forming the first cross-breed, it would be considerably reduced in its spiritual and cultural importance. But also, in this case, the product of the crossing would succumb in the mutual struggle for life, as long as there exists a higher race, that remained unmixed, as opponent. Any herd-like inner completeness of this new national body [*Volkskörper*], formed in the course of a thousand years, would nevertheless, in consequence of the general lowering of the race standard and the diminishing of mental elasticity and creative ability, conditioned by it, not suffice for overcoming victoriously the struggle with an equally uniform but spiritually and culturally superior race. (604)

Thus, according to Hitler, homogeneity of racial elements in the same nation made for national strength, heterogeneity of racial elements made for national weakness. The classical example of a heterogeneous nation was Germany. Originally a nation of pureblooded Germanic-Nordic stock, Germany absorbed many non-Germanic elements into its ethnic body. The German nation was no longer of pureblooded Germanic-Nordic race. Other race elements: "Easterners," "Dinarics," "Westerners," had become parts of the German nation. But these different racial components had never been thrown into the melting pot of a new race: "Unfortunately," wrote Hitler, "our German nationality [Volkstum] is no longer based on a racially uniform nucleus," but "the process of the blending of the various primal constituents has not yet progressed so far as to permit speaking of a newly formed race. . . . It is not a new race that results from the fusion, but the racial stocks remain side by side. . . . The racial elements are situated differently, not only territorially but also in individual cases within the same territory. At the side of Nordic people there stand Easterners, at the side of Easterners Dinarics, at the side of both stand Westerners, and in between stand mixtures" (597–98).

Throughout its history, asserted Hitler, waves of inferior races swept Germany, a "blood-poisoning which affected our national body [Volkskörper], especially since the Thirty Years' War" (597).[2] All that "led not only to a decomposition of our blood but also of our soul" (597). Different races lived side by side on German soil tearing it apart and causing it to lose the

2. The Thirty Years' War lasted from 1618 to 1648.

unity of its national will. Germany fell prey to a superindividualism which found its historical expression in extreme particularism, *i.e.*, the continued existence of independent principalities rather than one united nation.

Hitler considered Germany's lack of racial homogeneity the curse of the past because, in his words, "this side by side placement of our basic racial elements which remained unblended" deprived the German people of its herd instinct, of its unified national will. Hitler believed that had Germany possessed this herd instinct, the old Imperial German Reich would have achieved world domination and would have brought peace unto the world—a peace under the wings of the German eagle. "If, in its historical development," he declared,

> the German people [*Volk*] had possessed this group unity as it was enjoyed by other peoples, then the German Reich would today be the mistress of this globe. World history would have taken a different course, and no one would be able to decide if in this way there would not have arrived what today so many blinded pacifists hope to beg for by moaning and crying: *A peace, supported not by the palm branches of tearful pacifist professional female mourners, but founded by the victorious sword of a people of overlords [Herrenvolk] which puts the world into the service of a higher culture.* The fact of the non-existence of a nationality [*Volkstum*] uniform in its blood. . . . has bereft the German people [*Volk*] of its right of mastery. (598–99)

However, Hitler suggested, the fact that the racial strains remained unblended, so detrimental in the past, held the great promise of the future. "That which has brought us misfortune in the past and in the present," he said,

> can be our blessing in the future. For no matter how detrimental it was on the one hand that a complete mixture of our original racial constituents did not take place, and that by this the formation of a uniform national body [*Volkskörper*] was prevented, it was just as

fortunate on the other hand, that by this at least a part of our blood was preserved in purity and escaped racial decline.

With the complete blending of our original racial elements a closed national body [*Volkskörper*] would certainly have ensued, but, as every racial cross-breeding proves, it would be endowed with an ability to create a culture inferior to that which the highest of the primal components possessed originally. This is the blessing of the failure of complete mixture: that even today we still have in our German national body great stocks of Nordic-Germanic people who remain unblended, in whom we may see the most valuable treasure for our future. (599–600)

In this manner Hitler argued that the political and cultural mastery in the world which Germany forfeited in the past because of her lack of racial uniformity, was actually no "loss." Germany, as a crossbred nation, might have conquered the world, but she would not have been able to fulfill her cultural mission in history. The great opportunity to become the "noblest" race would have been lost forever. Fortunately, it seemed to Hitler, great reserves of that "noble" stock still existed in Germany, sufficient to carry through a program of biological renaissance of the nation. By newly promoting the Germanic-Nordic stock, Germany could and would regain her original purity and avail herself of the historic certainty to become the "Mistress of the globe." The historic mission that Hitler assigned to the Third Reich was, therefore, not confined to unification of all people of German race into one state and the extension of the German racial frontiers into a new lebensraum, but as well it presupposed the purification of the race. With all these conditions fulfilled, Hitler believed the German Reich could and would rise to world rulership. He wrote:

Today we know that a complete intermixture of the stocks of our natinal body [*Volkskörper*], in consequence of the unity resulting from this, would perhaps have given us external power, but that the highest goal of mankind would not have been attained, as the only bearer whom Fate has visibly elected for this completion would have perished in the general racial mixture of a uniform people [*einheitavolk*].

But today, from the viewpoint of our knowledge now gained, we have to examine and to evaluate what, without our contribution, has been prevented by a kind destiny.

He who speaks of a mission [continued Hitler] of the German people [*Volk*] of this earth must know that it can exist only in the formation of a State which sees its highest task in the preservation and the promotion of the most noble elements of our nationality [*Volkstum*] which have remained, even of the entire mankind, unharmed. . . .

The German Reich, as a State, should include all Germans, not only with the task of collecting from the people the most valuable stocks of racially primal elements and preserving them, but also to lead them, gradually and safely, to a dominating position. (600–601)

By this the State for the first time receives an inner higher goal. In the face of the ridiculous slogan of a safeguarding of peace and order for the peaceful possibility of mutual cheating, the task of the preservation and the promotion of a highest humanity which has been presented to this world by the benevolence of the Almighty, appears a truly high mission.

Out of a dead mechanism [wrote Hitler] that claims to exist only for its own sake, a living organism has now to be formed with the exclusive purpose of serving a higher idea. (601)

This task had a double aspect: first, the negative measure of eliminating the dysgenic elements in the nation: "He who is not physically and mentally healthy and worthy must not perpetuate his misery in the body of his child;" second, and positively: "the conscious methodical promotion of the fertility of the most healthy bearers of the nationality [*Volkstum*]" (608, 609).

Hitler declared that only this "racially most valuable nucleus of the people"—healthy stock and Nordic stock Hitler obviously assumed to be more or less identical—should be entrusted with the settlement of lebensraum. He wrote:

> The way towards this is above all that the State does not leave the settlement of newly won land to chance, but that it subjects it to special norms. Specially formed race commissions have to issue a certificate of settlement to the individual; but this is dependent on a certain racial purity, to be established. Thus frontier colonies can gradually be formed whose inhabitants are exclusively bearers of highest racial purity and with this of highest racial efficiency. They are a precious national (*national*) treasure of the entire people [*Volksganzes*]; their growth must fill every national member [*Volksgenosse*] with pride and joyful confidence, as in him there lies the germ for the ultimate great future development of their own people [*Volk*], even of mankind. (609–610)

Hitler posed the goal of Germany's cultural leadership against what he considered "the ridiculous slogan of the safeguarding of peace and order for the peaceful possibility of mutual cheating," which had been the ideal of the Wilhelmian empire with its talk of peaceful economic conquest. Not pacifism, but continual attack was the watchword for the future:

> Therefore, in the place of a fundamentally stabilized condition appears a period of fighting. But as everywhere and with everything in this world, here too the phrase 'who rests—rusts' will keep its validity, and further, that victory is forever contained only in attack. The greater thereby the fighting goal that we have in mind, and the less the understanding of the great masses may be at the moment, the most enormous are, according to world history, the successes—and the importance of these successes if the goal is rightly understood and the fight is carried out with unshakable persistency. (601–602)

In this great future of the German people, predicted Hitler, the "*superindividualism*" which taken all in all "has deprived us of world domination," will no longer be an obstacle. Such a fighting Germandom, he maintained, of the racial morrow will have the "sure herd instinct" without being subject to the danger of cultural decadence which inevitably would have followed the hybridization of the "Nordic-German" in the general mixture of a uniform people (598–600).

Obviously, for Hitler, the final stage of racial "purification" could be achieved only over a period of generations. It would be wrong, however, to draw the conclusion that Hitler, while writing *Mein Kampf*, inferentially ruled out the possibility of German world domination during his lifetime. Hitler found readily at hand an able agency of unification in the Prussian state and above all in the Prussian army, which in the German past had proven capable of artificially overcoming, at least partially, the disintegrating tendencies rooted in Germany's racial heterogeneity. Hitler considered "the organization by the Hohenzollerns of the Brandenburg-Prussian state as a model and crystallization nucleus of a new Reich" (941), one of the great achievements of German history. The creation of the Prussian state precipitated the cultivation

of a special State conception, as well as of the bringing into organizational form and adaptation to the modern world of the German army's impulse of self-preservation and self-defense. The transformation of the individual defense idea into national defense duty [*Wehrpflicht der Nation*] sprung from this State structure and its new State conception. The importance of this development cannot in the least be exaggerated. Precisely the German nation [*Volk*], super-individualistically disintegrated because of its jumbled blood, regained from discipline through the Prussian army organism, at least in part, the capacity for organization which it had long missed. What is aboriginally present in other nations [*Völker*] as a result of their herd instinct, we artificially reacquired for our national community [*Volksgemeinschaft*], at least partially, through the process of military training. (942)

In the existence of Prussia, Hitler found the clue to the short-cut which otherwise would have taken generations to fulfill:

the state of the Hohenzollerns, with all its shortcomings, merely by means of the Prussian army, succeeded in restoring to the German people, extrinsically, the minimum of unity. Why then should not the "Third Reich," by carrying through the organizational integration of the different German states (Bavaria, Prussia, Brunswick, etc.) in one reich and by using the Prussian military organism with its iron discipline and its leadership principle, succeed in imposing a uniformity of will upon the nation strong enough to overcome the centrifugal forces of the blood? By virtue of such an "emergency" solution, world domination could yet be placed on the agenda of the present instead of a far-distant future.

Hitler's play upon the time factor was one of the most interesting psychological methods for making his thousand-year reich appear as a vision of transcendant value. At the same moment he gave the living Germans the assured hope of actually coming into this reich. He affirmed this hope by glorifying and reawakening the spirit of Potsdam with all its trimmings, from goose step to the glory of war.

Hitler believed that once a fighting Germany, endowed with a healthy and increasingly unified racial stock and led by a state which was the "sovereign incorporation of a nation's [*Volkstum*] instinct of preserving itself on this earth" (602) had gained world domination, then—and ony then—could world order be based on pacifism.

> He who actually desires [he wrote], with all his heart, the victory of the pacifistic idea in this world would have to stand up, with all available means, for the conquest of the world by the Germans. . . . Therefore, whether one wanted to or not, if one had the serious will, one would have to decide to wage war in order to arrive at pacifism. . . .
> . . . Indeed, the pacifist-humane idea is perhaps quite good whenever the man of the highest standard has previously con-

quered and subjected the world to a degree that makes him the only master of this globe. Thus the idea is more and more deprived of the possibility of a harmful effect in the measure in which its practical application becomes rare and finally impossible. Therefore, first fight, and then one may see what can be done. (394–95)

Hitler rejected every idea of cooperation of equal nations through federation in Europe or in the world. He rejected every idea of community or a league of nations. World hegemony and domination by one superior nation was the one possible solution of international integration whereby the nations of kindred race (Aryans) could occupy the preferential positions. He assigned racial kinship the task of ruling over inferior races.

It is necessary to deal here with one more question in order to make clear the relationship of Germany to the Aryan world in Hitler's system. We know of Hitler's eager concern for the future of the Aryan race. What to him is the final court of appeals: the interests of the Aryan or the interests of Germany? The answer may be summed up as follows: Germany's Herculean labors were to be expended first and above all in the struggle for victory, power, position of Germany. But Germany's final triumph resulting in world rulership would at the same time assure the final victory of the Aryan race. The Aryan peoples would live peacefully together protected by the sword of Germany. Germany would be the arbiter of the world.

But in the era that preceded the establishment of the Aryan millennium national clefts necessarily remained within the Aryan world. Fratricidal wars might become inevitable, for in Hitler's words "kinship relations among nations cannot at all eliminate rivalries" (903). It is with reference to this period of transition to world domination that Hitler warned the German youth not to confuse dream ideas of Aryan world brotherhood with the interests of Germany, not to become the knights-errant for other nations, be they Aryan or non-Aryan. "The folkish movement," he asserted, "must not be the attorney for other nations, but the vanguard fighter of its own. Otherwise it is superfluous, and especially has no right to beef about the past. For then it is acting like the past. Much as the old German policy was improperly determined from dynastic viewpoints, equally little must the future be governed by dreamy folkish cosmopolitanism. Above all, however, we are not protective police for the well-known 'poor little nations,' but soldiers of our own nation" (950). Only in the eschatological promise of an Aryan millennium under Germany's aegis, predicted Hitler, would that conflict between the narrower racial group, called the German nation, and the wider racial group of the Aryans find its solution. Not until then would there be world peace and a new era of world culture.

Hitler magnanimously took pains to identify the interest of a world-conquering Germany with the interests of mankind. He asked, what has the world to gain from "the victorious sword of a people of overlords?" Is it only the promised relief from the scourge of the war, the blessings of a world peace? No, Hitler claimed to bear gifts more "precious" than the "Pax Germanica," namely an unprecedented cultural development of the world. This new epoch of world culture would be again, in its essential character, an Aryan culture. Since time immemorial, Hitler declared, it was the Aryan who was the creator of all culture. "What we see before us of human culture today, the results of art, science, and techniques, is almost exclusively the creative product of the Aryan" (397). For, Hitler decreed, culture by definition is Aryan culture. The Aryan "is the Prometheus of mankind, out of whose bright forehead springs the divine spark of genius at all times, forever rekindling that fire which in the form of knowledge lightened up the night of silent secrets and thus made man climb the path towards the position of master of the other beings on this earth. Exclude him—and deep darkness will again fall upon the earth, perhaps even, after a few thousand years, human culture would perish and the world would turn into a desert" (398).

Hitler assigned to the Germans, the "people of overlords," not only the political, but also the cultural leadership among the Aryan peoples. Racially reborn, the German people would represent the noblest branch of the noblest race, the Aryans. The Nordic-Germanic stock was to be the rock upon which Hitler hoped to build the future Germany, "the germ for the ultimate great future development of their own people, even of mankind." In this sense Hitler conceived the mission of Germany to lead the world on the path to the Aryan culture of tomorrow.

According to Hitler it fell upon the Germans to put "the world into the service of a higher culture." This formulation obviously implied the idea of an enslavement of inferior races in the service of the Aryan culture. Such an inference was warranted not only by Hitler's general attitude toward the inferior races; it rested also on his description of the origins of Aryan cultures: it was only by the slave labor of the inferior races that the early Aryan cultures were sustained.

It is no accident [he wrote] that the first cultures originated in those places where the Aryan, by meeting lower peoples, subdued them and made them subject to his will. They, then, were the first technical instrument in the service of a growing culture.

With this the way that the Aryan had to go was clearly lined out. As a conqueror he subjected the lower peoples and then he regulated their practical ability according to his command and his will and for his aims. But while he thus led them towards a useful, though hard activity, he not only spared the lives of the subjected, but perhaps even gave them a fate which was better than that of their former so-called 'freedom.' As long as he kept up ruthlessly the master's standpoint, he not only really remained 'master' but also the preserver and propagator of the culture. For the latter was based exclusively on his abilities, and with it, on his preservation in purity. (405–406)

Hitler believed that as long as the Aryan kept his conscious racial superiority and asserted his mastery, culture flowered, even to the benefit of the slaves. But once the Aryan master race gave itself over to the delusion of equality and lowered the racial barriers, its doom was sealed. The Aryan blood fused with that of the inferior slave races.

But [argued Hitler] as soon as the subjected peoples themselves began to rise . . . the sharp separating wall between master and slave fell. The Aryan gave up the purity of his blood and therefore he also lost his place in the Paradise which he had created for himself. He became submerged in the race-mixture, he gradually lost his cultural ability more and more, till at last not only mentally but also physically he began to resemble more the subjected and aborigines than his ancestors. For some time he may still live on the existing cultural goods, but then petrifaction sets in, and finally oblivion. (406)

Hitler in formulating a general law of history that culture is Aryan culture, warned Aryan mankind. "Historical experience offers countless proofs of this," he wrote. "It shows with terrible clarity that with any mixing of the blood of the Aryan with lower races the result was the end of the culture-bearer" (392). "For the people do not perish by lost wars, but by the loss of that force of resistance which is contained only in the pure blood. All that is not race in this world is trash. All world historical events, however, are only the expression of the races' instinct of self-preservation in its good or in its evil meaning" (406).

II

Hitler believed that new land and purification of the race would open the road for the Germans to become the leading nation in the world. But in his mind there existed an antagonist throughout the world—the Jew. Jews, Hitler believed, had strangled the nations of the world and were preparing to make true their age-old dream of world domination.

"The Jewish State," he wrote, "was never spacially limited in itself." The Jewish people have always formed "a State within other States" and made this state "sail under the flag of religion." The Jew is the great "master of lying," Hitler continued, the pure egoist who lives as a parasite in and off the body of other peoples and states. His chief means to enter the national bodies are racial and civil equality, religious tolerance, free press, and above all, democracy. To destroy national unity by class struggle a Jew invented Marxism. Yet to reign internationally, economic and financial power has to yoke in the nations by international treaties and pacifist institutions—all this in order to win real world power by spreading Jewish-Russian bolshevism throughout the world. But the Jew can never hold world power because of his innate destructive nature. He destroys everything in his way and is bound to destroy himself eventually.

Hitler's fantasy of a growing Jewish menace transformed the Jew into a metaphysical abstract, "the personification of the Devil." He described the Jew as the main danger to the Aryan world—to the purity of the Aryan races. The Jew became the prime antagonist of Aryanism. The Aryan was the creator; the Jew was the destroyer. For, declared Hitler, "the Jew possesses no culture-creating energy whatsoever, as the idealism, without which there can never exist a genuine development of man towards a higher level, does not and never did exist in him. His intellect, therefore, will never have a constructive effect, but only a destructive one . . . Any progress of mankind takes place not through him but in spite of him" (418).

Hitler insisted that the possession of enormous economic power as well as the age-old consciousness of being the selected people impelled the Jew. He wrote, "the higher he climbs, the more alluringly rises out of the veil of the past his old goal, once promised to him, and with feverish greed he watches in his brightest heads the dream of world domination step into tangible proximity" (430). In this manner, Hitler imagined that the Jew continuously schemed for world domination. After the Napoleonic War princes and their mistresses tried to divide the world among themselves. Today, argued Hitler, it is the Jew who bids for world domination. "Moreover, times have changed since the Congress of Vienna: princes and the mistresses of princes do not barter and haggle about frontiers, but the implacable world Jew is struggling for dominion over the nations. No nation can dislodge this fist from its throat except by the sword" (946).

The political significance of Judaism in modern times, however, suggested Hitler, began with the emergence of the Jew from the ghetto. First, he tried to remove his political disability. So far he had been deprived of his civil rights and citizenship on religious grounds. The maintenance and further expansion of his economic empire alone made it imperative that he be treated as equal in society, Hitler asserted. "His financial rule of the entire business life has already progressed so far that, without the possession of all the 'civil' rights, he is no longer able to support the whole enormous building, in any case no further increase of his influence can take place" (430). As an entering wedge the Jew cunningly used the Freemasons. "For the strengthening of his political position," wrote Hitler, "he tries to pull down the racial and civil barriers which at first still restrain him at every step. For this purpose he fights with all his innate thoroughness for religious tolerance—and in the completely deteriorated Freemasonry he has an excellent instrument for fighting out and also for 'putting over' his aims. By the strings of Freemasonry the circles of the government and the higher layers of the political and economic *bourgeoisie* fall into his nets without their even guessing this" (433).

Accordingly, the Masonic orders were employed by the Jew to inveigle the upper classes. To beguile the common man the Jew used, Hitler declared, another, coarser instrument, the press. For

> one cannot catch glovemakers and linen weavers in the fine net of Freemasonry; for this one has to apply more coarse but not less thorough means. Thus to Freemasonry the second weapon in the service of Jewry is added; the *press*. He puts himself into possession of it with all toughness, but also with infinite versatility. With it he begins slowly to grasp and to ensnare, to lead and to push the entire public life, because now he is in a position to produce and to conduct the power which under the name of 'public opinion' is better known today than it was a few decades ago. (433–34)

While in his press, Hitler continued, the Jew preached all those ideals that destroyed race consciousness and national values, the Jew himself anxiously guarded the purity and solidarity of his own race. Wrote Hitler, "While he seems to overflow with 'enlightenment,' 'progress,' 'freedom,' 'humanity,' etc., he exercises the strictest seclusion of his race. Although he sometimes hangs his women onto the coattails of influential Christians, yet he always keeps his male line pure in principle. He poisons the blood of the others, but he guards his own. The Jew does not marry a Christian woman, but always the Christian a Jewess. Yet the bastards take to the Jewish side" (434).

Meanwhile the Jew exercised his newly won influence to

prepare the way for democracy. Democracy, Hitler theorized, was based on the principle of majority, and subversive to national strength. The weaker the national will, the easier the way to Jewish world domination. The victory of democracy was therefore, the goal of the Jew in this particular phase of his march to world rule. "His final goal in this state [phase], however," declared Hitler, "is the victory of 'democracy,' or as he understands it: because it eliminates the personality—and in its place it puts the majority of stupidity, incapacity, and last, but not least, cowardice" (435–36).[3]

While still working for the promotion of democracy, Hitler argued, the Jew was already busy preparing for bolshevism, the next and last stop on his march towards the hoped-for world domination. The Jew became the theorist and organizer of the labor movement. As the era of industrial revolution opened, the Jew cleverly sensed the great political energies which lay dormant in the dissatisfied working class, and slyly he seized the unlimited opportunity for the future that was offered here (439). The Jew wormed his way into the confidence of the workers, and appealing to their Aryan sense for social justice, he aroused the "have-nots" against the "haves" by way of the Marxian doctrine:

> He approaches the worker [Hitler asserted], pretends to have pity on him, or even to feel indignation at his lot of misery and poverty, in order more easily to gain his confidence in this way. He takes pains to study all the actual (or imagined) hardships of his life— and to awaken a longing for changing such an existence. In an infinitely sly manner, he stimulates the need for social justice, dormant in every Aryan, to the point of hatred against those who have been better favored by fortune, and thus he gives the fight for the abolition of social evils a definite stamp of a view of life. He founds the Marxist theory. (440)

3. The English translation contains a printing error—in capitalizing the word *state*—which we have eliminated. *State* is here used in the sense of *phase* (*Stadium*).

Hitler insisted that the Jew repeated the same trick he had used before when he capitalized on the class struggle between the bourgeoisie and the feudal class. But now the stake he gambled for was infinitely greater. Before his goal was merely full civil rights, now it is rulership. The new proletarian class would serve as his vehicle.

> As soon as, out of the general economic transformation, the new class develops [Hitler predicted], the Jew sees also before him, clearly and distinctly, the new pacemaker of his own further advancement. First he uses the bourgeoisie as the battle ram against the feudal world, then the worker against the bourgeois world. Just as at one time he knew how to gain by sneaking the civil rights for himself in the shadow of the bourgeoisie, thus he hopes now that in the worker's fight for his existence, he will find the way towards a leadership of his own. (439–40)

Hitler imagined the Jews to be playing a diabolically clever game. With the one hand the Jew organized the capitalist exploitation of the workers; with the other hand he organized the exploited against the capitalists. He led the workers against himself. But this

> 'against himself' is, of course, only metaphorically expressed, for [Hitler claimed] the great master of lies knows how to make himself appear always as the 'pure' one and to charge the guilt to the others. As he has the impudence to lead the masses in such a manner, the latter does not even think at all that this could mean the most villainous betrayal of all times. . . .
> . . . From now on the worker only has the task of working for the future of the Jewish people. He is unconsciously put into the service of that power which he believes he is fighting. By making him apparently storm against capital, one can most easily make him fight just for the latter. Thus one always cries out against international capital, whereas in reality one means the national economy. The latter is to be demolished so that on its field of carnage the triumph of the international stock exchange may be celebrated. (439, 440)

Hitler insisted that the stronghold from which to rule the world was international finance. He argued that stock exchange Jewry entered the single states and tried to internationalize them in order to dominate the economic and national life. "Jewry," Hitler declared,

> will always fight within particular national bodies with those weapons which seem most efficient and promise the greatest success in the light of the well-known mentalities of these nations. Consequently, in our body national, so jumbled from the viewpoint of blood, it uses in its struggle for power the pacifist ideological conceptions sprung from these more or less 'cosmopolitan,' in short, international, tendencies; in France it employs the well-known and well-understood chauvinism; in England, economic and imperial conceptions; in short, it always utilizes the most essential characteristics exhibited by a people's mentality. Only when by such means it has added a certain luxuriant influence to its wealth of economic and political power does it slough off the hobbles of this transferred weapon and now equally advance the true inner intent of its will and struggle. It begins ever more quickly to destroy, until it thus transforms one State after another into a mass of ruins, on the basis of which shall later be established the sovereignty of the eternal Jewish empire. (906–907)

Hitler believed that the greatest progress the Jews made toward world cultural decay and at the same time toward world domination occurred close toward the end of the first World War. He wrote, "In Russian bolshevism we must see Jewry's twentieth-century effort to take world dominion unto itself, just as it sought to strive towards the same goal in other periods by other, if inwardly related doings" (960). Jewish bolshevism, by uprooting the Germanic elements, destroyed the Russian empire, which owed its existence not to the "inferior" Russian race, but to the "Germanic nucleus of its superior strata of leaders." "In the surrender of Russia to bolshevism," declared Hitler, "the Russian people was robbed of that intelligentsia which theretofore produced and guaranteed its State stability. For the organization of a Russian State structure was not the result of Russian Slavdom's State-political capacity, but rather a wonderful example of the State-building activity of the German element in an inferior race" (951).

According to Hitler the Jew took the place of the Germanic leadership, but since the strength of the Jewish race lay only in destruction, it would be unable to maintain its rule over Russia. Soviet Russia was, therefore, bound to collapse, although not from inner revolts alone.

> Impossible as it is for the Russians alone to shake off the yoke of the Jews through their own strength [asserted Hitler], it is equally impossible in the long run for the Jews to maintain the mighty empire. Jewry itself is not an organizing element, but a ferment of decomposition. The Persian Empire, once so powerful, is now ripe for collapse; and the end of Jewish dominion in Russia will also be the end of the Russian State itself. We have been chosen by Fate to be the witnesses of a catastrophe which will be the most powerful substantiation of the correctness of the folkish theory of race. (952)

Hitler predicted that the next great goal of Jewish bolshevism was Germany. He wrote, "Germany is today the next great battle aim of bolshevism" (961). "The internationalization of our German economy, i.e., the passing of German labor power into the possession of Jewish world finance, can be carried not only in a politically bolshevised State" (905). "The Jewish train of thought is, moreover, clear. The bolshevization of Germany, i.e., the extermination of the national folkish intelligentsia and the exploitation of German labor power in the yoke of world Jewish finance facilitated thereby, is thought of solely as a preliminary to a further extension of this Jewish tendency to conquer the world" (906).

Hitler argued that thus Germany became the pivot in the world struggle between Aryanism and Judaism. But Hitler believed that Jews had to be defeated all over the world. "Thus," he wrote, "as so often in history, the mighty struggle within Germany is the great turning-point. If our people and our State fall victims to this bloodthirsty and moneythirsty Jewish tyrant over nations, then the whole world will fall into this polyp's net; if Germany frees itself from this embrace, this greatest of all dangers to the nations can be regarded as crushed for the entire world" (906). This fight against Jewish bolshevism and international finance was for Hitler one of the great historic tasks of the Germans. Thus, the prevention of Jewish world power with all its institutions, from world finance and Freemasonry to democracy, was the real war aim of Hitler.

According to Hitler, Germany had to begin by cleansing her own body of "Jewish parasites." It is one of the elements of Hitler's foreign policy to free his allies from the Jewish influence. Hitler regarded the destruction of Jewry as one of his main war aims. On the other hand Hitler used this incipient battle against the Jews as one of the major tools in his propaganda in order to awaken and revolutionize the Germans. To Hitler "at all times, the efficiency of the truly national leader consists primarily in preventing the division of the attention of a people, and always in concentrating it in a single enemy" (152). By telling the masses that the Jew was the driving force behind Marxism, democracy, Freemasonry, international finance capital, the League of Nations, French imperialism, and Russian bolshevism—all these enemies were brought under a common denominator. Hitler wrote:

> It is part of the genius of a great leader to make adversaries of different fields appear as always belonging to one category only, because to weak and unstable characters the knowledge that there are various enemies will lead only too easily to incipient doubts as to their own cause.

As soon as the wavering masses find themselves confronting too many enemies, objectivity at once steps in, and the question is raised whether actually all the others are wrong and their own nation or their own movement alone is right.

Also with this comes the first paralysis of their own strength. Therefore, a number of essentially different internal enemies must always be regarded as one in such a way that in the opinion of the mass of one's own adherents the war is being waged against one enemy alone. This strengthens the belief in one's own cause and increases one's bitterness against the attacker. (152–53)

Little wonder that the Jewish question was given such broad scope in *Mein Kampf*. In the subject index of the German edition of *Mein Kampf*, the references listed under "Judaism" occupy almost a page; only the references listed under the heading of "National Socialism" occupied more space in the index.

Hitler did not bother to mention that the myth of the "chosen people" was developed in Judaism. To avoid this comparison, Hitler shunned the term "chosen people" but nonetheless utilized the concept in a distorted form.

III

Hitler had clearly indicated as his positive war aims the new German world order and as his negative war aims the destruction of the present national institutions and world relations dominated and shaped, as he saw it, by Jewish machinations. Hitler explained the conditions under which the Germans could take upon themselves this gigantic task. He had opened their eyes to the historic opportunity from the racial as well as from the geographical point of view to become the dominating nation. But his total system was still not closed and conclusive; he had to convince himself and the Germans of the righteousness of the means and the justification of the ways to fulfill these tasks—namely by ruthless war. He revealed to the Germans that the right means were predetermined by the "law of nature," *i.e.*, the right of the stronger to subdue the weaker. According to *Mein Kampf*, violence—from the concentration camps to the battlefield—was the method sanctioned by the law of nature or, as Hitler termed it, "by the law of progress of mankind."

Hitler had imagined that lebensraum would guarantee a healthy balance between industry and agriculture by settling increasing numbers of those of pure German blood. "Destiny" had left to the Germans the historical opportunity to become a pure nation, unified and strong by virtue of sound herd instinct. He believed that it was fortunate for the Germans that they had not mixed their Nordic stock with inferior races in order to obtain, as a new, thoroughly crossbred national unity—at the cost of a lower level of blood and culture. Thus, according to Hitler, the remaining Nordic stock had the potential basis of a new, purified German nation determined to become "the noblest branch of the noblest race." Such a purified nation had to fulfill the great mission to create and fashion a new Aryan culture. He declared that an awareness of mission must exist in the heart and mind of every young German. This awareness had to be complemented by the moral call to act accordingly. Every young German should be possessed by the indomitable will to power and the stamina to pursue hard struggles for continuous conquest.

Hitler devoted much thought to determining the means to attain this. He found the answer by looking to nature. In the "law of nature" Hitler found the rationale to gain power and utilize it continuously with ruthless force. He justified this mode of life by the "aristocratic" right of the stronger to dominate the weaker. He found this first principle of nature and of history in the expression "the Eternal Will that dominates this universe to promote the victory of the better and stronger," and thereby the demand of "the submission of the worse and the weaker" (580).

This is quite obviously a crude restatement of Darwin's survival of the fittest. In fact, Darwinian influence is prevalent in Hitler's weltanschauung. Hitler adhered to the principle of evolution: "The progress of mankind resembles the ascent on an endless ladder; one cannot arrive at the top without first having taken the lower steps" (405). This evolution was interpreted by Hitler in a teleological fashion, as progress. He spoke of "Nature's will to breed life as a whole towards a higher level" (390). For Hitler the transcendent terms *creator*, *eternal will*, and *nature* were metaphysical entities by which universe, nature, and culture are determined.

According to Hitler the better and stronger proved his worth in the crucible of the struggle for existence. "Nature"— as a teleological force—presided over this permanent selection by conflict which was intended by her as the prime organ of natural as well as social history. The struggle for existence, *i.e.*, the survival of the fittest, was the agency of all progress in nature as well as in human history. What we find here is a very crude projection from the natural into the social sphere of Darwin's evolutionary hypothesis and of the Darwinian struggle for existence. At the same time Hitler clothed the will to power with an ethical justification. For if it is asserted that the victory of the strongest is the dynamic to which the program of mankind is due, ethical sanction is bestowed on the urge to power, conquest, and domination.

The aristocratic law of nature as accepted and promulgated by the Nazis implied the preordained fundamental inequality of races and individuals. Hitler saw in it not only the "different values of the races, but also the different values of individual man" (580). In other words, Hitler advanced the proposition that the militant selective principle operated in the struggle between race and race as well as between the individuals within each race. From that the führer principle was derived.

On the basis of the preordained inequality of races Hitler categorically asserted a hierarchy of races. Thus the Aryan, by virtue of natural endowment, was superior to the Jew, to the Negro, to the Mongoloid races, and the Nordic, again, was superior to all other Aryans. Human races were considered as species with fixed immutable characteristics. Hitler implied that nature had divided the organic world into species and willed the preservation of their identity; i.e., the purity of races or species. In the animal kingdom, he asserted, every animal of a given species complies with that "brazen basic principle" of Nature. "Every animal mates only with a representative of the same species. The titmouse seeks the titmouse, the finch the finch, the stork the stork, the field mouse the field mouse, the common mouse the common mouse, the wolf the wolf, etc." (389).

Hitler admitted exceptions to that rule, "but then Nature begins to resist this with the help of all visible means." Nature protests against such a violation of her will in two forms: either she limits or denies to the bastard offspring the procreative faculty, or "she takes away the capacity of resistance against disease or inimical attacks" (390). Confronted, in the struggle for existence, with a representative of the higher standard, crossbred races go down in defeat. In this way nature preserves the immutability of the species.

Hitler declared that a mating between higher and lower species was a blatant violation of the "aristocratic" law of nature because, he wrote, it "contradicts Nature's will to breed life as a whole towards a higher level. . . . The stronger has to rule and he is not to amalgamate with the weaker one, that he may not sacrifice his own greatness. Only the born weakling can consider this as cruel . . . for, if this law were not dominating, all conceivable development towards a higher level, on the part of all organically living beings, would be unthinkable for man" (390).

For Hitler any hybridization violated the aristocratic thought of nature. "The result of any crossing, in brief," he said, "is always the following: (a) Lowering of the standard of the higher race, (b) Physical and mental regression, and, with it, the beginning of a slowly but steadily progressive lingering illness. To bring about such a development means nothing less than sinning against the will of the Eternal Creator" (392).

This law applied to all living beings from the titmouse to the Aryan; it applied to individuals and races alike. He explained, "Just as little as Nature desires a mating between weaker individuals and stronger ones, far less she desires the mixing of a higher race with a lower one, as in this case her entire work of higher breeding, which perhaps has taken hundreds of thousands of years, would tumble at one blow. Historical experience offers countless proofs of this. It shows with terrible clarity that with any mixing of the blood of the Aryan with lower races the result was the end of the culture-bearer" (392). Therefore, "the man who misjudges and disdains the laws of race actually forfeits the happiness that seems destined to be his. He prevents the victorious march of the best race and with it also the presumption for all human progress, and in consequence he will remain in the domain of the animal's helpless misery burdened with the sensibility of man" (397).

It becomes clear from the foregoing quotation that "the victorious march of the best race" is not taken by Hitler as a foregone conclusion. If the Aryan peoples allowed themselves to be bastardized or to be blinded by pacifism, the earth might still fall prey to lower races that have preserved their pristine fighting qualities and aggressive spirit.

As, unfortunately only too frequently, the best nations, or, better still, the really unique cultured races, the pillars of all human progress, in their pacifistic blindness decide to renounce the acquisition of new soil in order to content themselves with 'domes-

tic' colonization, while inferior nations know full well how to secure enormous areas on this earth for themselves, this would lead
to the following result:

The culturally superior, but less ruthless, races would have to
limit, in consequence of their limited soil, their increase even at a
time when the culturally inferior, but more brutal and more natural, people, in consequence of their greater living areas, would be
able to increase themselves without limit. In other words: the
world will, therefore, some day come into the hands of a mankind
that is inferior in culture but superior in energy and activity.
(174–75)

For Hitler there was therefore no comfortable and safe way
charted by Providence for the Aryan. If the Aryan lost his urge
for self-preservation, he would be doomed. For, Hitler claimed
that "in the end, only the urge for self-preservation will eter-
nally succeed. Under its pressure so-called 'humanity,' as the
expression of a mixture of stupidity, cowardice and an imagi-
nary superior intelligence, will melt like snow under the
March sun. Mankind has grown strong in eternal struggles
and it will only perish through eternal peace" (175). Hitler despised pacifists because they were at variance with the design
of the "Creator" to set up a pacific world with the palm. A
peaceful world, according to Hitler was only possible as long
as a superior race could preserve its strength to subjugate
the other races. World peace was a militant peace based on
"the victorious sword."

There is a strong activist volitional element in Hitler's
theory of struggle for existence. Nature favored the better and
the stronger, but no race had a prior claim to the title of the
"chosen" race. Every race and nation had to prove its worth in
the eternal race struggle. The whole surface of the earth was
the arena in which this struggle was fought. Frontiers were
man-made. They were not sacred and inviolable by nature's
sanction. On the contrary, he wrote, "Nature did not reserve
this soil in itself for a certain nation or race as reserved terri-

tory for the future, but it is land and soil for that people which has the energy to take it and the industry to cultivate it. Nature does not know political frontiers. She first puts the living beings on this globe and watches the free game of energies. He who is strongest in courage and industry receives, as her favorite child, the right to be the master of existence" (174).

* * *

Mein Kampf contains a theory of the workings of nature and, at the same time the inner meaning of history. "Inequality" of the nations and individuals and "purity" of races to accomplish perfection and survival were, according to Hitler, the two great maxims on which nature and history were bound to develop according to the intention of the "Creator." In explaining that the eternal "laws of nature" were simultaneously "laws of history" Hitler claimed to have discovered the meaning of history—the past and the future. Hitler's race concept is not a biological concept only. It asserts that specific innate qualities of specific races enable specific deeds to be accomplished in political and cultural development as well.

For Hitler "culture" was only "Aryan culture." In opposition to "so-called scientists" and experts of "so-called democratic" nations, Hitler "proved" from the pages of history that only purest Nordic stock was endowed to create the highest culture. He insisted that only the Germans had the chance and precondition to fulfill such a "mission." The "Creator" had predetermined the condition (*i.e.,* purity) and the end (*i.e.,* new world culture) attainable under those given conditions. Adolf Hitler had offered his guidance in showing the equally predetermined right means. What was left to the Germans by way of self-determination was the will to fulfill the conditions and to avail themselves of the right means—and the ends would be theirs.

What were these exclusive right means? Nature created unequal specimens. Unequals faced tests and trials on this earth, and only the better and stronger survived. On the basis of this aristocratic law of nature, Hitler developed the "law of progress" in history. Progress resulted from trials and tests, rose from battlefields and bloody sacrifices. The continuation of progress was guaranteed by the domination of the fittest and the subservience of the weaker. The purified Germans had to undergo this ordeal of the "becoming"—since no other way led to progress and world peace. To live up to their predestination, Hitler declared, Germans must be willing to use ruthless power as well as to bring great sacrifices. By such tremendous efforts the Germans signified their choice to become the "chosen" people.

4 ⌖ The Political Structure of a Future Nation

We know that Hitler's intention was to wipe out democracy in this world. In the following chapter we shall become acquainted with Hitler's political philosophy on race, state, and führer, which provides the principles of the future political structure of his vision of the Aryan nation. Hitler never dealt explicitly with the form and the structure of the new world order. Knowing his logical system, we may reasonably deduce from the foregoing some positive as well as negative implications regarding underlying principles which Hitler observed consistently to install the political props and the institutional frame for this new world.

Hitler visualized a qualitative hierarchy of nations according to their racial composition. The leading German nation would work together with the other Aryan nations who would divide the world into interest spheres among themselves. Accordingly, races would become subservient in every respect. There would be no League of Nations in which small and big powers would share equal rights and duties and cooperate on this basis at a common task. Hitler argued that such a set-up merely serves inferior stocks to tip the scales against the superior powers. Hitler would definitely and forever do away with the alleged "Jewish menace of world domination" and the "Jewish world finance power" that he imagined to be lodged in the bastions of Wall Street and the city of London.

85

He would abolish the Jewish-Bolshevist threat. In his utter contempt of the "atomistic" liberal world-exchange system Hitler made it clear that the new division of labor would be based on the relation between the dominating Aryan countries to the inferior nations—a network of interrelated economic and political dependencies; the needs of the leading nations would determine the economies of those dependent nations. The general principles of his future world policy, although visible, are yet vague in outline. The final and concrete blueprint of the relationship among the nations would be offered after the "housewarming party" of world conquest.

Today Hitler's intentions are clearer with regard to the economic and political structure within the individual nations. In his "political philosophy," which was designed, above all, for the German people, Hitler laid down the "model" ideas of the functional interrelationship between race or nation, and the state and the economy. Hitler has dealt at length with the rotten systems of "so-called" democracies, with their pernicious overgrowth of individualism on the one side, which sets to nought every stirring of community spirit, and their ossified rule by sheer majorities on the other.

Hitler's ideas on foreign and domestic policy are consistent with one another. The basic ideas which Hitler applied to the world at large were at the same time the basic ideas guiding the inner order of the German nation.

Hitler accepted two basic axioms, namely purity or homogeneity of race, which guarantees national unity, and inequality and heterogeneity of races or nations, which lead to ultimate domination by the stronger and better. Hitler says clearly that the aristocratic principle of nature is valid for the individual too: The Eternal Will favors "the fundamental aristocratic thought of nature and believes in the validity of this law down to the last individual. It sees not only the different value of the races, but also the different values of the individual man."[1] But there is a great difference between applying the principles of inequality and unity among nations in the world and applying them within one given nation.

For Hitler, among the nations, inequality of the nations and unity (purity) of the Nordic master race were complementary principles; in the impact of the two principles upon each other, world conquest could be reached. But within one nation unity and inequality were competitive and in essence antagonistic, even mutually exclusive, principles if they were demanded and applied 100 percent. In fact, no unity can exist in the anarchy where individualism rules absolutely. Hitler, however, recognized these incompatabilities and the difficulty involved. If he applied the same two axioms as the basic principles of his political philosophy within the nation, he decided clearly that the higher and decisive value lies in the race and not in the individual. He assigned absolute value to the community of physically and psychically kindred, *i.e.*, racially equal, human beings. Only on the basis of this kind of equality are individual differentiations admitted. "Just as in general," he wrote, "I have to evaluate the nations differently on the basis of the race to which they belong, thus also the individuals within a national community. The statement that a people is not equal to a people is then transmitted to the individual within a national community in the sense that a head cannot be equal to a head, because here too the elements of the blood may be the same, in great lines, but in individual cases are nevertheless subject to thousandfold, most minute differentiations" (660). Within the national community there are the racially equal but individually gifted ones with their differential qualities.

1. Adolf Hitler, *Mein Kampf* (New York: Reynal and Hitchcock, 1939), 580, hereinafter cited in the text by page number only.

Democracy and Marxism violated this aristocratic principle of nature. "The parliamentary principle of decision by majority," declared Hitler, "by denying the authority of the person and placing in its stead the number of the crowd in question, sins against the aristocratic basic idea of Nature" (103), and "Marxism, indeed, presents itself as the perfection of the Jew's attempt at excluding the overwhelming importance of the personality in all domains of human life and of replacing it by the number of the masses" (666). "A human community appears well organized only if it makes the work of these creative forces easier in the most complying manner and applies them for the profit of the community" (665).

Here Hitler identified a new difficulty, namely "to recognize, in the community of all, those heads that are mentally and ideally most valuable indeed, and to give them that influence which not only is due these superior minds, but which above all is beneficial to the nation. This sieving according to ability and efficiency cannot be carried out mechanically, but it is a work that is done uninterruptedly by the daily struggle for life" (661). "Many break and perish, thus proving that they are not chosen for the ultimate, and only a few appear finally as selected. In the fields of thinking, of artistic creation, even of economy, this process of selection still takes place today, though especially in the latter it is exposed to a serious handicap. State administration and the power of the nation, as incorporated in the organized army, are equally dominated by this idea" (665–66).

Hitler believed that the leadership principle pervaded every phase of national and social life. It was modeled after the Prussian army. "The State," he wrote,

> in its organization, beginning with the smallest cell of the community up to the highest leadership of the entire Reich, must be built upon the principle of personality. There must be no decisions

by majority, but only responsible persons, and the word 'council' is once more reduced to its original meaning. At every man's side there stand councillors, indeed, but one man decides. The principle which once made the Prussian army the most marvelous instrument of the German people has to be some day in a transformed meaning the principle of the construction of our whole State constitution: authority of every leader towards below and responsibility towards above. (669–70)

Hitler called his ideal political state order based on the leadership principle "Germanic democracy." He then contrasted this "genuine" democracy with the "sham" democracy based on parliamentarianism and majority, behind which he saw the influence of the Jews. "It is not the object of our present-day democratic parliamentarianism," Hitler declared,

> to form an assembly of wise men, but rather to gather a crowd of mentally dependent ciphers which may be more easily led in certain directions, the more limited the intelligence of the individual. Only thus can parties make politics in the worse sense of the word today. . . .
> With this, however, all responsibility is practically removed, because it can only be the duty of an individual and never that of a parliamentary assembly of babblers. . . .
> Therefore, this kind of democracy has become the instrument of that race which shuns the sunlight because of its internal aims, now and for all time. Only the Jew can praise an institution that is as dirty and false as he is himself. (115–16)

Hitler asserted that the organizing principle of Aryan mankind was "the true Germanic democracy of the free choice of a leader with the latter's obligation to take over fully all responsibility for what he does or does not do. There will be no voting by a majority on single questions, but only the decision of the individual who backs it with his life and all he has" (116–17). The logic of the principle that demanded that the best were to be selected for the right places, in practice, called

for the building up of an "elite." "This principle of unconditional connection of absolute responsibility with absolute authority," he stated, "will gradually breed up a choice of leaders
as is inconceivable today, in the era of irresponsible parliamentarianism" (671). And again, "A view of life which, by re-
jecting the democratic mass idea, endeavors to give this world
to the best people, that means to the most superior men, has
logically to obey the same aristocratic principle also within
this people and has to guarantee leadership and highest influence within the respective people to the best heads" (661).

Hitler argued that the "elite" was naturally crowned by "the
Führer": He wrote, "out of the host of sometimes millions of
people, who individually more or less clearly and distinctly
guess this truth, partly perhaps understand it, one man must
step forward in order to form, with apodictic force, out of the
wavering world of imagination of the great masses, granite
principles, and to take up the fight for their sole correctness,
until out of the playing waves of a free world of thought a brazen rock of uniform combination of form and will arises. The
general right for such an activity is based on its necessity, the
personal right, in success" (577). The masses of the people,
though inert, blind, and without a grasp of the deep problems
of history and nature that are understandable only to the
Führer and the élite, were just the same a part of "nature" and
therefore instinctively wished for the victory of the stronger
man. "The great masses are only a part of nature," affirmed
Hitler, "and this feeling does not understand the mutual hand-
shake of people who assert that they want various things.
What they want is the victory of the stronger and the annihilation or the unconditional surrender of the weaker" (469).

Hitler envisaged the same hierarchical order in the political
set-up of the nation as existed in his party. The interplay between Hitler's idea, the leader, the advisors, the members,

and the followers in the party corresponded to the interplay of the staggered political forces within the nation (namely, the imposed doctrine, the leader, the elite, and the masses). When Hitler came to power he slipped over onto the whole nation the political structure that he had previously developed and tested out in the party. Thus, the party system with its hierarchical structure, was the skeleton for the new German political body.

In addition, however, the party tried to permeate and to control the entire complex of German social institutions. This control of the party, exercised over those parts of the people that were not absorbed by Hitler's system as such, constituted the essence of Hitler's political dictatorship. However, it should be borne in mind that the leadership principle with its hierarchical structure did not, as such, mean dictatorship, but a new political structure. According to Hitler, dictatorship, with its Gestapo apparatus of control and enforcement, had to be followed only as long as the leadership principle did not emerge organically out of the whole nation. This presupposed the universal recognition of the dogma.

Undoubtedly, the hierarchical leadership principle did not fulfill what Hitler promised, namely, the rise of the most qualified people to the positions they merited. It is clear that under this narrow-minded dogma imposed by Hitler, the most broad-minded and scientifically schooled people would cease to enter the race for leading positions in the nation for which they would be qualified. They left it to the less able or to the opportunists to become their over-zealous leaders. Under such conditions, even the élite that was to council the Führer had become an assemblage of mediocrities.

According to Hitler's "political philosophy," the political organization of the "folkish" community of German people united by the ties of race was the state. With that, the nature of the state was instrumental or functional, not absolute. Hitler did not join what a popularizing concept calls the Hegelian worship of the state per se. In Hitler's words: "We must sharply distinguish between the State as a vessel and the race as the content. This vessel has meaning only if it is able to preserve and to protect the contents; in the reverse case it is useless" (595). For his state was endowed with two essential tasks: the preservation of the racial stock and the "free" development of all the great abilities in the nation.

> The State is a means to an end [he wrote]. Its end is the preservation and the promotion of a community of physically and psychically equal living beings. This very preservation comprises first the racial stock and thereby it permits the free development of all the forces slumbering in this race. Again and again a part of them will primarily serve the preservation of the physical life and only another part will serve the promotion of a further mental development. But actually the one always creates the presumption for the other.
>
> States that do not serve this purpose are faulty specimens, even miscarriages. The fact of their existence makes as little difference as perhaps the success of a filibuster community is able to justify robbery. (594–95)

He continued, "The German Reich, as a State, should include all Germans, not only with the task of collecting from the people the most valuable stocks of racially primal elements and preserving them, but also to lead them, gradually and safely, to a dominating position" (601). "The folkish State. . . . has to put the race into the center of life in general. . . . the State has to appear as the guardian of a thousand years' future, in the face of which the wish and the egoism of the individual appears as nothing and has to submit" (608).

Hitler gave first place to the purely political aspects and not to economic considerations proper, which often influence politicians and laws in "so-called" democratic countries. For Hitler, politics takes precedence in determining the economic action of the individual. As the state is the servant of the race, so the national economy is the servant of the state. "Capital is not master of the State, but its servant."[2] He wrote:

> The State has nothing whatsoever to do with a definite conception of economics or development of economics.
>
> The State is not an assembly of commercial parties in a certain prescribed space for the fulfillment of economic tasks, but the organization of a community of physically and mentally equal human beings for the better possibility of the furtherance of their species as well as for the fulfillment of the goal of their existence assigned to them by Providence. This, and nothing else, is the purpose and the meaning of a State. Economy is, therefore, only one of the many auxiliary means necessary for reaching this goal. (195–96)

In this way, Hitler believed, the political and economic order of a nation must be blended into a functioning unit. The economic interests of individuals could only be sanctioned by the state in which the individual existed. The welfare of the individual was necessarily dependent on the state. In light of such a concept of the relation between state and individual interests, the controversy of capitalism versus socialism no longer existed. He declared, "the highest form of Nationalism finds its expression only in an unconditional devotion of the individual to the people. It will never be denied that the purest form of socialism means the conscious elevation of the claims of the people, its life and its interests above the interests and the life of the individual. But it is a task '(of a real statesman)' of immeasurable difficulty to translate the recognition of these facts from the world of ideals, from the sphere of abstract thought, into the realms of hard actualities."[3]

Hitler's socialism, as we shall see, has nothing but its name

2. Adolf Hitler, Speech of April 24, 1923, in Ernst Boepple (ed.), *Adolf Hitler's Reden* (Munich: Deutscher Volksverlag, 1933), 59.

3. Adolf Hitler, *My New Order*, ed. with commentary by Raoul de Roussy de Sales (New York: Reynal and Hitchcock, 1941), 282.

in common with the socialism of the labor movement. Socialism, even before Marx, was generally understood to be the abolition of capitalism as an economic system and of a social order of inequality in which the means of production were in the hands of a few private individuals. Private ownership of the means of production was to be replaced by the ownership of the new society. National socialism, in contrast, acknowledged private property in principle and placed it under the protection of the state, even as it denied expressly the idea of equality of rights. Moreover, Hitler introduced the leadership principle throughout the whole economic structure. The individual managers of enterprises were the responsible leaders of that enterprise not as capitalists for their own benefit only, but as leaders for the benefit of the community of the plant as well as indirectly for the larger community.

This leadership principle of the managers and businessmen was one of the most apt psychological and legal means for safeguarding the domination of the state's interest over the different and unequal individual interests. As the party program of the twenty-five points stated in point 10: "It must be the first duty of every citizen of the State to work with his mind or body. The activities of the individual must not clash with the interests of the whole, but must be pursued within the framework of the national activity and must be for the general good."[4]

An example of how the hierarchical order worked in practice was that, in spite of the fact that the German businessman was called the "leader" of his enterprise and as such was held responsible to government, he had become more or less an agent of the state even before the outbreak of this war. He was controlled economically and politically in his own enter-

4. Michael Oakeshott, *The Social and Political Doctrines of Contemporary Europe* (Cambridge: Cambridge University Press, 1939), 191.

prise—from above, from below, and from all sides. In his own enterprise the Labor Front disputed his decisions and watched him politically. He had to be a member of the various compulsory business organizations, which to a large extent were supervised by the party and, in any case, by the government. Not least, he was controlled with regard to quality, quantity, and prices of his products, and his customers. Above all, his investments and the hiring and firing of his workers were regulated by the innumerable governmental agencies.

In contrast, under the Weimar Republic the German businessman, with the support of his own business associations and cartels, still had possessed the means to make himself heard by the government directly as well as in public. He was able to make such decisions in his factory as he deemed fit, even to limit or abandon his business. Therefore, the governmental bureaucracy had to gain the cooperation of businessmen with regard to the economic measures it suggested or, as in the field of labor, to establish institutions designed to mediate between freely organized labor and freely organized entrepreneurs.

Yet even before the war, under Hitler, representatives of business could scarcely influence the economic policy—Nazi party and governmental bureaucracy had become the decisive factors. In essence the Nazis nationalized the entrepreneurial function and frequently left business with nothing to do except carry the risk. In fact, businessmen developed a new function, namely, to find the loopholes in the network of restrictions or to gain party support, which, although costly, yielded profits. Still, the vital armament industries were able to maintain a position of preference, supported as they were by the relatively independent military bureaucracy.

In general, the Nazi rule that individual business interest had to be subordinated to the common good was carried into practice so thoroughly that the independent businessmen disappeared. Instead a new species of businessman emerged in the form of agents and managers who persistently tried to regain influence with regard to their business interests through the various channels of the Nazi party. The changed relation between state and economy created a new type of man.

5 卐 Strategy and Tactics
in Foreign Policy

Knowing Hitler's frenzied hatred of bolshevism, the world could not comprehend the sudden cooperation with Russia at the beginning of this war. However, Hitler's adherents or readers of his principles of foreign policy could understand the whys and hows of this tactical move. On the other hand, with regard to his policy for England, Hitler caught himself in his rigid foreign policy strategy. The real war aims of Hitler became the doctrine of the young soldiers. Their minds were trained in the understanding of the war aims on the basis of Hitler's fundamental axioms laid down in *Mein Kampf*. This textbook had yet another purpose, namely, to develop in the minds of the adherents a new method of considering and organizing problems, particularly of foreign policy, in a new functional way. Foreign policy was invariably, for Hitler, power policy. For him it was oriented by his now so often described goals. In the service of this leitmotif, the first task of statecraft was to recognize the enemies—those nations whose fundamental interests were a bar to his expansion of power.

The second task of statecraft was to find nations who were naturally opposed to his enemies and who, therefore, could be won over to add their power to his own expansionist interest. Alliances meant for Hitler "a joint expansion of power." He wrote:

Alliance policies are not advanced from considerations of backward-looking discords, but rather fructified by a knowledge of past experiences. Experience, however, should now have taught us that alliances for the achievement of negative goals suffer from internal weaknesses. National fates are solidly welded together only through a perspective of a common triumph, in the sense of common gains, conquests, in short, a joint expansion of power. . . .

. . . The premise for the linking of national fates never lies in mutual respect or even congeniality, but in a perspective of mutual expediency for both contracting parties. That is, let us say, however invariably an English statesman pursues pro-English policies and never pro-German, quite definite interests of these pro-English policies can, for the most diverse reasons, duplicate pro-German interests. This, of course, need be the case only to a limited degree, and can in time turn into the exact opposite: the skill of a leading statesman shows itself solely in exactly this, always to find for the achievement of his own needs in a specified period that partner who, for the advocacy of his own interests, must follow the same course.[1]

In order to distinguish between an actual enemy and a prospective ally Hitler undertook a lengthy analysis of the power constellation after the first World War. He lined up the nations likely to be favorable or unfavorable to his aims. He weighed the political influence and the military strength of both sides, but still more, he subjected their population trends, their geographical situations, and above all, their racial compositions to scrutiny. On the basis of his findings of the prevailing power constellation and under the aspect of utility to himself, Hitler developed his long-range strategy. He lined up the nations with common interests against his enemies as allies. As he explained, "Practical application for today can, consequently, mean only: which States at the moment have no vital interest in French economic and military

1. Adolf Hitler, *Mein Kampf* (New York: Reynal and Hitchcock, 1939), 901–902, hereinafter cited in the text by page number only.

power achieving an absolute ruling position of hegemony by means of the total elimination of a German Middle Europe" (902). Hitler stipulated his desired British-Italian-German entente as the ideal "axis" for the "predictable future" (908).

But the realist in Hitler acknowledged circumstances which called for what we may term tactical moves or, better, detours.[2] For example, Germany's tie-up with the most inferior race of Russia was such a deviation from his "principled" power policy. For Hitler it meant an undesirable but unavoidable detour. To be sure the Soviet-German nonaggression pact of 1939 was signed with full mutual distrust and misgivings on the part of both. Hitler's adherents understood at once the ephemeral value of this pact with Russia. They had learned to see Hitler's foreign policy in its totality and, therefore, knew how to distinguish between strategy and tactics. For if only adherents and followers of a movement were fully absorbed by the guiding goal and understood the nature of the "principled" foreign policy by which to reach this goal, they would easily consent, and with malicious approval, to the most paradoxical, yet tactical, maneuvers.

Theoretically, Hitler was well aware of the fact that favorable or unfavorable shifts in the power constellation would demand changes in his strategy. He acknowledged in principle that the attainment of one step toward his final goal might necessitate a reexamination of alliances to determine whether the next step had to be executed with new partners. He took great satisfaction in conjuring up the ghost of Bismarck, for whom a political course was never "a matter of eternal principle" (953). Yet in practice Hitler never basically changed his strategy after he wrote *Mein Kampf* nor the picture of desir-

2. The term *tactics* as employed here and throughout this chapter is used by Hitler interchangeably to signify strategic measures as well as "detours" within the strategic plan.

able allies he had once formed in his mind. He did change his tactics, as we know from the case with Russia. His strategy was too much bound up with other, particularly the racial factors to permit political expediencies to prevail. Hitler was continually exposed to the implications of his own bias that inferior races could be considered as trusted allies from the strategic point of view. Thus, for instance, his prejudiced analysis of the natural interests of England as opposed to France continued to be valid for him up to the time when the events immediately after Munich might have taught him better. It is quite conceivable that Hitler even today thinks of England as a natural ally with regard to his world conquest and especially in his fight against the United States.

The first step in Germany's rise to the status of a "world power" had to be action towards "unification of all Germans" into a single Reich. It goes without saying that this demand included the *Anschluss* of Austria and the incorporation of the Sudetenland. The unification policy was for Hitler a matter of course. He was fully convinced of his right of action and, even more, of the forthcoming support of world opinion. Thus Hitler's reasoning about his future foreign policy was guided primarily by his second goal, *i.e.*, the annexation of lebensraum. He wrote, "we must again profess the advocacy of the supreme point of view of every foreign policy; that is: to bring the land into consonance with the population. . . . Soil and territory [must be] the goal of our foreign policy" (943–44).

This strategy toward lebensraum demanded, first, a strengthening of Germany's war potency, so that Germany might again have something with which to entice other nations to seek her cooperation. "Can a power," Hitler asked, "which seeks in an alliance help for the achievement of its own offensive goals, tie itself to a State whose leaders for years present a picture of the most pitiful incompetence and pacifist cowardice . . . ?" (903)

Second, this achievement at the same time engenders a fundamental change in the European power constellation, a work of far-sighted diplomacy leading to new alignments of power blocks. Germany would regain her "prestige" as a world power. On that basis alone would the unification of the Germans in Great Germany be facilitated.

Third, the result of both, including war perhaps, would lead to Germany's hegemony in Europe, which could be upheld only by lebensraum. In a world crystallizing into large-scale nations and empires only a contiguous Reich with far-flung frontiers could give Germany definite and real world-power status. Hitler revealed to the world in 1927 this line of his strategy when he wrote his "political testaments."

> The political testament of the German nation for its dealing with the outside world, however, should and must always read substantially:
> Never tolerate the establishment of two continental powers in Europe. See an attack on Germany in any attempt to organize a military power on the frontiers of Germany, be it only in the form of the creation of a State capable of becoming a military power, and, in that case, regard it not only a right, but a duty, to prevent the establishment of such a State by all means including the application of armed force, or, in the event that such a one be already founded, to repress it. (963)

This "political testament" clearly implied that Germany had to attain and then jealously guard her monopoly as the dominant military power on the continent.

Hitler's analysis of the power situation of postwar Europe today belongs to history. The historian may smile at the simple and grotesquely primitive manner in which Hitler treated the difficult and complex question of foreign relations after the first World War. However, to us who are engaged in the fight against Hitler, it must be of the greatest importance to see how far his unsophisticated analysis is bound up with his

fanatically conceived goals viewed under the same, constantly reiterated, aspects of race value and race history. In this respect Hitler's analysis of the role of France in Europe is highly
instructive.

To determine the power constellation most favorable for the
strengthening of Germany and, later on, for her hegemony,
Hitler put his finger on France as the paramount danger for
Germany. France's hegemony over the continent was well-
nigh complete. Rooted in the system of alliances, France had
built up in central and eastern Europe a diplomatic supple-
ment to the Maginot Line. Germany's way to lebensraum was
thus barred. As a matter of logic, this road could be cleared
only by destroying France as a power in Europe. The relationship with France consequently became one lever of Hitler's
foreign policy. He declared, "the future goal of our foreign policy" should be "an eastern policy signifying the acquisition of
the necessary soil for our German people. Since we need
strength for this, but the mortal enemy of our nation, France,
relentlessly throttles us and robs our strength, we must un-
dertake every sacrifice which may help to bring about a nul-
lification of the French drive for European hegemony" (966).

It is a general belief that Hitler's stand against France was
little more than the traditional *Erbfeind* ideology of the German nationalist and of the bourgeois jingoist whose anti-
French foreign policy saw its supreme goal in "revenge." But
for Hitler the elimination of France solely as a major military
or colonial power was not an end in itself but a means to the
acquisition of lebensraum.

Hitler frankly admitted, "Much as we all today recognize
the necessity for a reckoning with France, it will remain
largely ineffective if our foreign-policy aim is restricted there-
to. It has and will retain significance if it provides the rear
cover for an enlargement of our national domain of life in Eu-

rope" (949). "Germany really sees in France's destruction a means of subsequently and finally giving our nation a chance to expand elsewhere" (978–79).

Yet Hitler shared, to a certain degree, the view that France's power was the cause of Germany's eternal political frustration. He wrote, "Because we must at last become entirely clear about this: the German people's irreconcilable mortal enemy is and remains France. It does not matter who ruled or who will rule in France, whether Bourbons or Jacobins, Bonapartists or bourgeois democrats, clerical republicans or red Bolsheviks, the final goal of her foreign-policy activity would always be an effort to hold the Rhine frontier and to guarantee this stream by means of a disintegrated and dismembered Germany" (902).

Hitler gave an even more convincing argument why, since the middle of the last century, France had had a vital reason to keep Germany down. "Only through the obliteration of Germany," declared Hitler, "can a France, which is slowly withering, not only in its population figures, but especially in its racially best elements, maintain its world importance in the long run" (978). As an alternative to Hitler's plan, French and German politicians had kept discussing a new order in Europe in terms of a firm economic and political alliance between France and Germany.

This solution was actually attempted by the great statesmen Aristide Briand and Gustav Stresemann; they envisioned an eventual overcoming of the nationalistic, militaristic, and chauvinistic oppositions in their countries and a firm cooperation in bringing to rest the continuous clashes among European countries. France was to guarantee the financial stability of the eastern countries, while Germany, as the great industrial producer and consumer of foodstuffs and raw materials was to build an economic exchange system embracing the

East. On such a financial and economic basis the European peace would rest securely. Finally, they intended to initiate a European spending program for railways and utilities in the eastern countries which was to raise their standard of living and, in addition, give industrial exports to France and particularly Germany.

But Adolf Hitler resented the very idea of an alliance with France as a sign of weakness and irresponsible blindness because of the racial quality of the French people. With a racially mixed people such as the French, no constructive alliance should ever be contemplated by Germans. Hitler asserted, "This people, which is constantly becoming more negrofied constitutes, by its tie with the aims of Jewish world dominion, a grim danger for the existence of the European white race. For infection in the heart of Europe through negro blood on the Rhine corresponds equally to the sadistic perverse vengefulness of this chauvinistic, hereditary enemy of our people, and to the ice-cold plan of the Jews thus to begin bastardizing the European continent at its core and, through infection by inferior humanity, to deprive the white race of the foundations for a sovereign existence" (907–908).

Since France was for this reason "the most terrible enemy," for Hitler the question was how to eliminate this stumbling block in the path of his goals and for the sake of the "existence of white humanity." This could be done only by allying Germany with any power ready to join in that aim, even at the price of German sacrifices. He wrote, "Every power which, like us, finds intolerable France's aspiration to dominion over the continent, is today our natural ally. No path to such a power must seem too difficult to us and no renunciation must seem unspeakable if the end result only offers the possibility of subduing our most enraged enemies" (966). All efforts, Hitler believed, must be bent toward this end. Germany "must not fall into the errors of the pre-War period and make enemies of everybody in the world, but it must recognize the most dangerous enemy in order to strike him with all its concentrated force" (917).

In the early twenties a German-English-Italian bloc appeared to Hitler as the most favorable system of alliance to achieve his aim of destroying France. He said in *Mein Kampf*, "For Germany, however, the French danger means an obligation to subordinate all considerations of sentiment, and to reach out the hand to those who, threatened as much as we are, will not tolerate and bear France's drive toward dominion. In Europe there can be only two allies for Germany in the predictable future: England and Italy" (908). Such an alliance "would give Germany a chance to make quite calmly those preparations which, one way or another, must be undertaken within the bounds of such a coalition for a reckoning with France" (964). He affirmed, "The greatest world power of the earth and a youthful national State would constitute different premises for a struggle in Europe than did the putrid State corpses with which Germany had allied itself in the last war" (965). "On the soberest and coldest reflection, it is today primarily these two States, England and Italy, whose most natural self-interests, at least in all essentials, do not oppose the conditions of existence of the German nation, indeed, to a certain degree are identical with them" (903).

Hitler was prepared to make great sacrifices to gain England's favor (962). His belief in being able to win England for an ally was based on the deep-rooted conviction that the interests of England and France were fundamentally opposed. He warned his adherents that such alliances should not be repudiated for sentimental reasons of revenge. "However horrible the results of English war policy were and are for Germany," he wrote, "one must not ignore the view that there is today no longer a necessary English interest in crushing Germany, but that, on the contrary, England's desire must from year to year be increasingly for a limitation of the unbounded French drive for hegemony" (900–901).

England and France had fought for hegemony in Europe for over a century. In a speech made two years before the publication of the first volume of *Mein Kampf*, Hitler said, "England and France have been struggling for hegemony for one hundred forty years. Despite the predatory war they fought as allies, they remain to this hour old, embittered rivals."[3] And in *Mein Kampf* he wrote, "The ultimate goal of French diplomacy will always stand in opposition to the final tendency of British statecraft" (900).

Hitler saw in France's drive for hegemony in Europe a violation of "the traditional trend of British diplomacy . . . since the achievements of Queen Elizabeth" to prevent "by all means the rise of any great European power above the level of the general scale of magnitudes, and, if necessary, to crush it by military means" (895). Hitler, in five full pages, elaborated upon England's old effort "by roundabout means of balanced, mutually binding relations of power among the European States, to maintain and secure the necessary protection in the rear for big British aims in world politics" (895). He wished to prove that "for three hundred years the history of our continent was substantially determined by" this effort. "After the destruction of Spain and the Netherlands as great sea powers, the might of the English State concentrated itself against aspiring France, until finally, with the fall of Napoleon I, the hegemony danger to England of this most dangerous military power could be regarded as broken" (895).

According to Hitler the rise of Germany "because of its

3. Adolf Hitler, Speech of April 13, 1923, in Ernst Boepple (ed.), *Adolf Hitler's Reden* (Munich: Deutscher Volksverlag, 1933).

enormous industrialization" was the reason that England departed so far from her natural policy as to ally herself with France to crush Germany. This alliance could have been forestalled, Hitler held, if Germany had given up her commercial, colonial, and naval ambitions and had turned to the East. By 1918, however, with Germany eliminated as a power of any consequence, France had become the dominant political power on the continent of Europe. "France had seized the initiative," he wrote, "and could dictate to others. . . . In reality England did not achieve her war aim. The rise of European power above the balance of the European continental State system was not only not prevented, but was facilitated to a heightened degree" (898).

Hitler believed that France's power on the European continent was more than an impediment to Britain's balance of power policy; it was actually a military menace since her "coastline along a wide front lying opposite the life nerves of the British Empire" constituted a serious threat to England herself and to her empire. "Not only do English population centers constitute a worthwhile goal for aircraft and long-distance batteries," declared Hitler, "but British commercial traffic lines would also be most unfavorably exposed to submarine activity. A U-boat war, based on the long Atlantic coast as well as on the no less extensive stretch of French frontier region on the Mediterranean coasts of Europe and North Africa, would have ravaging effects" (899). "The military predominance of France weighs heavy on the heart of the British Empire" (903). "England can never desire a France which, by possessing the enormous western European iron and coal deposits, has the premises of a threatening world economic status" (902–903).

Hitler realized the obstacles in the way of an alliance with England. "The disparity between official or, better, traditional

British statecraft and the controlling Jewish stock exchange powers," he asserted, "reveals itself nowhere better than in the various positions adopted towards questions of English foreign policy. Jewish finance desires, in opposition to the interests of the British State's welfare, not only the thorough economic smashing of Germany, but also its complete political enslavement" (905).

Jewish finance is interested in France's hegemony because, Hitler argued, "only in France is there today more than even an inner unanimity between the plans of the Jew-controlled stock exchange and the desires of a chauvinistically oriented national statecraft" (907). Here Adolf Hitler showed the anti-Jewish policy within Germany in another aspect, namely as a vital constituent of his foreign policy. He believed that the annihilation of the Jewish power in Germany would strengthen the anti-Semitic trends in England, in the interest of England's own welfare. He stated:

> The struggle against this Jewish world danger will, moreover, also start at this point.
> And again precisely the National Socialist movement has its mightiest tasks to fulfill:
> It must open the eyes of the people concerning foreign nations and must over and over again recall who is the real enemy of our present world. In place of the insane hate for Aryans, from whom almost anything at all can separate us, people to whom, however, we are united by common blood or the main lines of a related culture, it must condemn to general wrath the evil enemy of humanity as the true creator of all suffering. (931)

Even in Italy, Hitler saw "the disparity between the conceptions of the better native statecraft and the will of world exchange Jewry" (907). Yet he insisted,

> In one State the existing State power can be regarded as so solidly stabilized, and so unconditionally at the service of national inter-

ests, that we can no longer speak of a really effective blocking of political needs by international Jewish forces. The struggle which Fascist Italy is carrying on, perhaps at bottom unconsciously (although personally I do not think this is the case), against the three main weapons of Jewry is the best omen that, if only indirectly, the fangs will be torn out of this super-State power. The prohibition of Masonic secret societies, the persecution of the super-national press as well as the continuous undermining of international Marxism, and, on the other hand, the steady fortifying of the Fascist State conception, will, in the course of years, enable the Fascist government to serve the interests of the Italian nation increasingly, without concern for the hissing of the Jewish world hydra. (927–28)

But most importantly, Italy's foreign situation as such made her into a friendly ally. In Hitler's opinion Italy's position in relation to France was hampered and threatened by French continental and North African supremacy. Italy, therefore, was the other natural partner for a Germany aiming to defeat France. He affirmed, "Italy, too, can and would not desire further reinforcement of French superiority in Europe. Italy's future must always lie in a development territorially centered in the Mediterranean Basin. What Italy pursued in the War was not really a desire to see France made greater, but rather the object of giving a death blow to her hated rivals in the Adriatic. Every added continental reinforcement of France means, nevertheless, a future restriction on Italy" (903).

As France was the number one enemy in the west, so Russia loomed as the natural enemy in the east. The armies of France's eastern vassals blocked Germany's path to the coveted eastern plains. Soviet power stood directly athwart the same path to lebensraum. For, in addition to Poland and other eastern countries, Soviet territory was included in the lebensraum. Since the idea of friendship with Russia was then (1927) advocated by many folkish circles, even in his own party, Hit-

ler tried to combat this sentiment. In a lengthy discussion of
all the pros and cons of a German-Russian alliance, Hitler
sounded the racial trumpet for the folkish ear. He held that it
would be a gigantic blunder to join with Russia (and with the
oppressed peoples of the British empire such as the Indians and
Arabs) against England. Inferior peoples, he was convinced,
would never storm the British citadel. "It is simply an impos-
sibility," he declared, "for a coalition of cripples to storm a
powerful State determined, if need be, to risk the last drop of
blood for its existence. As a folkish man, who estimates the
value of humanity on racial bases, I may not, simply because of
my knowledge of their racial inferiority, link my own nation's
fate with that of these so-called 'oppressed nations'" (957).

Hitler considered the Slavs of Russia still more inferior as
they were led by Jewish Bolshevists, those deadly enemies not
only of Germany, but of any Aryan civilization. He wrote,
"The struggle against Jewish bolshevization of the world requires a clear attitude toward Soviet Russia. You cannot drive
out the Devil with Beelzebub. If even folkish circles today are
smitten with an alliance with Russia, then let them merely
contemplate Germany and become conscious of what support
they are getting for their initiative. Or do folkish people lately
regard action which is welcomed and demanded by the international Marxist press as blessed for the German people?
Since when do folkish people struggle with a weapon which
the Jew offers us like a shield-bearer?" (961–62). Furthermore,
if ever the occasion should arise that a Russian-German alliance would be desirable, nobody could expect the Russian
Jewish Bolsheviks to keep their word. "The present rulers of
Russia," said Hitler,

> do not at all think of entering an alliance sincerely or of keep-
> ing one.
> We must never forget that the regents of present-day Russia are

common bloodstained criminals; that here is the scum of human-ity, which, favored by conditions in a tragic hour, overran a great State, butchered and rooted out millions of its leading intellects with savage bloodthirstiness, and for nearly ten years has exer-cised the most frightful régime of tyranny of all time. Nor must we forget that these rulers belong to a nation which combines a rare mixture of bestial horror with an inconceivable gift of lying, and today more than ever before believes itself called upon to im-pose its blood oppression on the whole world. We must not forget that the international Jew, who today rules Russia absolutely, sees in Germany, not an ally, but a State marked for the same destiny. But one does not conclude a treaty with someone whose sole in-terest is the destruction of his partner. Above all, one does not make them with parties to whom no treaty would be sacred, since they inhabit this world, not as the advocates of honor and truth-fulness, but as the advocates of lying, deceit, theft, rapine, and plundering. If anybody thinks of going into treaty ties with para-sites, this resembles a tree's efforts to conclude to its own advan-tage an agreement with a mistletoe. (959–60)

Although Hitler stated that "bolshevist parasites will never keep a contract," he mulled over the question whether Russia could eventually be of help in a clash with the West. It was the spectre of a two-front war that lead Hitler to consider the possible merits of a German-Russian coalition from a tactical, *i.e.,* a purely military, point of view. Hitler himself answered the question of the value of cooperation with Russia and he decided that the military weakness of Soviet Russia at that time (in the early twenties) could not offer effective support to Germany engaged in the west. "Considered purely militarily," he wrote,

in the event of a Germano-Russian war against western Europe, which would probably, however, mean against the entire rest of the world, the relations would be simply catastrophic. The strug-gle would proceed not on Russian but on German soil, without Germany being able to get from Russia even the slightest effective support. The present German Reich's instruments of power are so miserable and so impossible for an external fight that not even a border guard could be maintained against western Europe including England, and precisely the German industrial district would lie defenselessly abandoned to our opponents' concentrated weapons of attack. In addition, there lies between Germany and Russia the Polish State, reposing entirely in French hands. In the event of a Germano-Russian war against western Europe, Russia would have to subdue Poland before it could bring its first soldier to a German front. It is, however, not nearly so much a question of soldiers as it is of technical armament. . . . The universal motorization of the world, which in the next war will be overwhelmingly decisive in the struggle, could hardly be met by us. For not only has Germany itself remained shamefully far behind in this most important field, but with the little it has, it would have to support Russia, which even today can still not call its own a single factory in which can be manufactured a motor vehicle that really runs. (957–58)

Many writers who were dumbfounded by the Soviet-German nonaggression pact in September 1939 could never have read the foregoing passages in which Hitler realistically weighed the value of a German-Soviet alliance and based his negative conclusion in good part on the industrial and military strength of the late 1920s. It is astonishing, but true, that during the "war of nerves," with the outbreak of military hostilities drawing closer, Hitler managed to bewilder the whole world by the conclusion of the German-Russian nonaggression pact which he then advertised as a token of "eternal friendship and a durable peace" between the Third Reich and the Red empire. The world shook their heads over Hitler's inconsistency and irrationality in foreign policy and called him a most unprincipled opportunist. But they underestimated, among other factors, Hitler's immense gift for shrewdly exploiting a situation. Above all, they underrated his great cunning in dressing up a tactical detour as a fundamental change in his strategy. But in the ranks of his own adherents and of his followers, the Russian move was looked upon in its true import. To them the coalition with Russia was a truce only.

On the basis of his analysis Hitler considered his enemies France and Russia. It was the task of German foreign policy to deal with them one after the other. Hitler believed that he understood his allies (actual or potential), too. Of Italy's support in his long-run policy he was sure. Italy would do everything to help Hitler regain the position of a European as well as of a world power for Germany. Italy could be persuaded by compensations to ally herself with him for further successes. Hitler had, in one respect, a terrible time inducing Italy to become his ally and at the same time to defend his policy before his adherents and followers, to reunite all Germans in a Great Germany. The touchy spot was, of course, Tyrol. On the one hand, he held it out as a concession to Mussolini. He formulated this renunciation of Tyrol in a negative way. Hitler wrote, "it would be a crime to set the stakes of 200,000 Germans while approximately more than 7,000,000 languish under alien rule and the main artery of the German people flows through the playground of black African hordes" (917). (The latter is an allusion to Alsace-Lorraine.) On the other hand, he left it an open question whether he included Tyrol as a country to be regained as one of the "lost imperial territories" after having restored "political independence and power of the motherland." In fact, as we know, he settled the case with Mussolini in freighting the Tyrolian Germans to Germany and the lebensraum (911–17).

But the role of England remained the crucial problem in the pursuit of his long-run policy. Hitler counted firmly on England's opposition to the hegemony of France in Europe. He trusted England to side with Germany in order to restore Germany's prestige as a great European power. Yet he felt that England would be provoked by an overbalancing Germany in

Europe. Any threat of a German hegemony in Europe could lead to a direct conflict with England's particular political mission about which Hitler lectured: "Just as England's traditional political goals desired and required more or less a Balkanization of Europe, so those of France did a Balkanization of Germany. England's desire is and remains the prevention of the immoderate rise of any continental power to world political importance; that is, the maintenance of a fixed balance of power relation among European States; for this seems to be the premise of British world hegemony" (899).

Although Hitler made no precise statement regarding the possibility of an Anglo-German clash, the eventuality was acknowledged in a roundabout way which tried to dodge the unpleasant issue. Thus Hitler did not say explicitly that the strong aspirations of Germany toward hegemony inevitably meant a conflict with England. He desired, under all circumstances, to find a way out of such a dilemma and to secure a permanent balance of interests with England. And in this consideration of mutual Anglo-German interests, he envisaged a conflict with England might be avoided at a time when Germany started her reckoning with France. The century-old foreign policy of England requiring the Balkanization of Europe could cease—so Hitler hoped—to be a central issue for England if in the meantime the United States' rivalry on the seas threatened Britain's naval hegemony.

Hitler wrote of the American threat:

> A new mistress of the world seemed to be growing out of the former colonial country, the child of the great mother. It is understandable if England today re-examines her former alliances in anxious disquiet and if British statecraft stares with dread toward a time when it will no longer be said:
> 'England overseas,' but 'the seas for the Union.'
> The gigantic American State Colossus, with its enormous

wealth of virgin soil, is more difficult to attack than the wedged-in German Reich. If some time here, too, the dice shall roll for a final decision, England would be doomed, were she to stand alone. (929)

Hitler did not reason out what line of foreign policy he would pursue once he had become master in Europe. But this essential thing he knew: his "mission" determined him to dispute England's and the United States' positions in the world when finally he built up German world hegemony.

It is one of Hitler's most characteristic traits to think of Germany's rise to world power in terms of definite stages. Hitler is so utterly unconcerned with world opinion as to reveal bluntly that he wants English support to arm and strengthen Germany. He hoped that during the rearmament period the vulnerability of England's far-flung empire would keep England at least neutral if Hitler were to challenge French hegemony. Here lies the great mistake in Hitler's calculation of his foreign policy. In fact, England realized—though in the last minute—the deadly danger to herself of Hitler's political gamble.

6 ⚎ Cardinal Virtues of a Nazi: A New Type of Man

In briefly outlining the educational program of Hitler, it is not our intention to take issue with that program as such. The reader is merely to get an idea what kind of values and virtues Hitler deemed the most desirable in a young German. This scale of virtues amounts to a revaluation of those values that are valid in a humanitarian world. It is clear that the product of an education along such lines will be a type of man totally different from what we call a free, upright, honest human being. Hitler's type of man is capable of being obedient, faithful, and silent only within the group, but he is ruthless and ferocious against the outsiders and "heretics." Hitler's man is convinced that he conveys a benefit to people of different creed if he foists his belief on them by threat and tortures. For Hitler, in Max Weber's words, "the ethics of internal and external relations are categorically distinct."

Hitler outlined his educational program in a few sentences:

> The folkish State, through this realization, has to direct its entire education primarily not at pumping in more knowledge, but at the breeding of absolutely healthy bodies. Of secondary importance is the training of mental abilities. But here again first of all the development of character, especially the promotion of will power and determination, connected with education for joyfully assuming responsibility, and only as the last thing, scientific schooling.
>
> Thereby the folkish State has to start from the presumption that

a man, though scientifically little educated but physically healthy, who has a sound, firm character, filled with joyful determination and will power, is of greater value to the national community than an ingenious weakling. A people of scholars, when they are physically degenerated, irresolute and cowardly pacifists, will not conquer heaven, nay it will not even be able to assure its existence on this globe.[1]

For Hitler the main goal of education from the cradle to the army was the "healthy body." By the process of physical education the feeling of superiority was to be implanted into the characters of all young Germans. This individual self-confidence was to expand into self-confidence of the group, and later on into national self-confidence. He wrote, "It is precisely our German people, that today, broken down, lies defenseless against the kicks of the rest of the world, who need that suggestive force that lies in self-confidence. But this self-confidence has to be instilled into the young fellow citizen from childhood on. His entire education and development has to be directed at giving him the conviction of being absolutely superior to the others" (618).

It is the highest goal of physical education, continued Hitler, to awaken this feeling of superiority. Only thus is the German people able to abide by the "aristocratic law of nature." Self-confidence and the feeling of superiority in the single individual as well as in the nation created the striving for leadership. In addition every young man must be trained and must discipline himself to unfold his character qualities towards responsibility as leader of a group as well as towards obedience as a servant of a higher leader.

In the first place Hitler valued the superior spirit as the potential source of victory. "For what once led the German army

1. Adolf Hitler, *Mein Kampf* (New York: Reynal and Hitchcock, 1939), 613–14, hereinafter cited in the text by page number only.

to victory," he declared, "was the sum of the confidence which the individual and all in common had in their leaders. The confidence in the possibility of regaining its freedom is what will restore the German people. But this conviction can only be the final product of the same feeling of millions of individuals" (618).

Second, self-confidence of the individual was commuted into a strong community spirit which above all pervaded the groups of the Hitler Youth. Only in such groups composed of young Aryans could the herd instinct be propagated which guaranteed unity of action and the mutual enforcing of morale. In these groups there had to be developed on a small scale the herd instinct and the morale which, after generations, would be possessed by the whole German nation. As this spirit came to dominate these groups, the fulfillment of Hitler's ideas would not need to wait. They could be promoted on such a basis until the entire German nation had attained racial purity. From these groups Hitler selected his Special Guards who were trained as the type of the Nordic man and educated in the spirit of the doctrine laid down in *Mein Kampf*.

Finally, the army was to become the "university" for teaching national self-confidence. "Further, strengthened by the confidence in his own force, seized by the strength of the commonly experienced *esprit de corps*," wrote Hitler, "he has to gain the conviction of the invincibility of his own nationality" (621). Physical education and superiority feeling evoked blood-consciousness as well. If the young healthy German felt himself a member of a pure and strong racial community, he would observe the eugenic rules, so that he might contribute to the improvement of the inborn and hereditary qualities of his Nordic stock. Thereby he would help found the basis for a pure united nation.

As of secondary importance [said Hitler] the folkish State has to promote the modeling of the character in every way.

It is certain that the essential features of character are fundamentally formed previously in the individual: one who is egoistic is and remains so once and forever, exactly as the idealist, in the bottom of his nature, will always be an idealist. But between the completely shaped characters there are millions of a type that appear dim and unclear. The born criminal will be and remain a criminal; but numerous people in whom a certain tendency towards criminality exists can still be made valuable members of the national community by proper education; while on the other hand by bad education vacillating characters can grow into really evil elements. (621)

Hitler asserted, "Today the conscious development of good and noble character qualities at school is equal to naught. This, one day, will have to be emphasized in quite a different manner. Loyalty, willingness to sacrifice, and silence are virtues which a great people urgently needs, and their inculcation by education and training in school is more important than many of the things which now fill our curriculum" (623). The family, the school, the group, and the army alike were to teach obedience, which meant being silent, loyal, and willing to bear sacrifices.

Hitler affirmed that "at the head of the military education should stand what had to be attributed even to the old army as its highest merit: in this school the boy should be turned into a man; and in this school he should not only learn to obey, but also acquire the training for commanding later on. He has to learn to be silent, not only when he is blamed justly, but he has also to learn, if necessary, to bear injustice in silence" (620–21). Silence is a national virtue for preserving national secrets, as Hitler repeatedly emphasized. He wrote:

How often one complained, during the War, that our people knew so little how to be silent! How difficult this made it to guard even important secrets from the knowledge of the enemies! But one should ask oneself the question: Before the War, what did German education do towards training the individual for secrecy? Was not unfortunately even in school the little tattle-tale preferred to his more discreet comrade? . . . Irresponsibly dropped remarks are passed on just as light-heartedly, our economy is constantly injured by a careless giving away of important methods of production, etc., even quiet preparations for the defense of the country are made illusory as the people have not learned to be silent but spread everything. But in case of war this inclination to talk can even lead to the loss of battles and thus contribute considerably to the unfortunate end of a struggle. Here, too, one has to be convinced that what one has not practiced during youth one cannot exercise during old age. (622)

Hitler insisted,

Of highest importance is the training of will power and determination, as well as the cultivation of joy in taking responsibility. . . .

Unfortunately, even at school one puts more stress upon the 'repenting' confession and the 'contrite abjuration' by the little sinner than upon a frank admission. The latter even appears to many a public educator of today the most visible symptom of an incorrigible depravity, and so many a boy, in an incredible manner, is threatened with the gallows for qualities which would be of priceless value if they were the common good of an entire nation.

As some day the folkish State has to devote its highest attention to the education of will and determination, it has to implant joy in taking responsibility and courage for confession into the hearts of the young from their early years of life. (623, 625)

If one young Elite Guard today would have this courage of confession against Hitler, there would be little time left to "repent"; more likely he would pay for his courage on the "gallows." Here we see the selective character of Hitler's ethics.

With regard to scientific education Hitler had very definite ideas. He declared:

The shortening of the curriculum and of the number of hours . . .
will be of benefit to the training of the body, of the character, and
of will power and determination. . . .
    The second change in the scientific curriculum of the national
State has to be the following:
    It is a characteristic of our present materialized time that our
scientific education turns more and more toward the subjects of
natural science only, namely, mathematics, physics, chemistry,
etc. No matter how necessary this is for a time in which techniques and chemistry dominate in daily life and represent its
symptoms, at least as far as outwardly recognizable, it is just as
dangerous if the general education of a nation is always directed
exclusively at this. On the contrary, this education has always to
be an ideal one. It has to correspond more to the classic subjects
and should only offer the foundations of a later training in a special field. . . . The Hellenic ideal of culture, too should be preserved for us in its exemplary beauty. One must not allow the differences of the individual races to tear up the greater racial
community. The struggle that rages today involves very great
aims: a culture fights for its existence, which combines millen-
niums and embraces Hellenism and Germanity together. (630–31)

Hitler's ideally oriented counterbalance to one-sided formal
education means in essence nothing else but indoctrination
of youth with a one-sided racial interpretation of world history from Hellenism to Hitlerism.
    Hitler continued, "As the third point, the following has to
be considered in connection with scientific education: Also in
science the folkish State has to see a means for the promotion
of national pride. Not only world history, but the entire culture history must be taught from this viewpoint" (635).
    So much for Hitler's suggestion concerning school educa-
tion. Group education also had to convey respect for history
and enthusiasm for historical figures. "The movement," he
said, "has to promote respect for the personality by all means;
it must never forget that the value of all that is human is
rooted in the personal value, that every idea and every

achievement are the results of the creative force of a man, and that the admiration for the greatness is not only a tribute of thanks to the latter, but that it also winds a unifying band around the grateful" (488). It was the talk of the Nazi organization to fill the young man with zeal and fanaticism.

He wrote, "In the ruthless attack upon an adversary the people sees at all times a proof of its own right, and it perceives the renunciation of his destruction as an uncertainty as regards its own right, if not as a sign of its own wrong" (468 –69). Only this fanatic will of Hitler's adherents and the newborn German youth will move the German masses to continuous and united action. Besides, the fanatic expression of will and courage to fulfill the German "mission" will impress the foreign onlookers too. "A nation, then, will be regarded as fit for alliance if (in our case) government and public opinion equally fanatically proclaim and advocate the will to struggle for freedom. This, then, is the first presumption for beginning the transformation of public opinion in other States, which, because of their understanding of their very own interests, are willing to march next to the partner who seems to them appropriate to these interests, that is, to make an alliance" (923–24). And "a people's ability to form alliances is far less determined by a dead lot of existing arms than by the visible presence of a flaming will of self-preservation and heroic death-defying courage" (461).

Group training with its strong emphasis on physical education, Hitler claimed, would fortify these values and virtues which were to be characteristic for a new German generation. Certainly many were called but not all were selected to comprehend fully and intellectually the reasonings of Hitler's *Mein Kampf*. Some had to carry the idea consciously in its cogent totality; others had to be carried along emotionally. Thus the idea either in one form or the other, had to guide the young soldier to and through the battlefield.

To recapitulate what a young Nazi must have thought as he marched into Poland:

1. The kinship of the blood demands one flag and one Reich for all Germans. The dictate of Versailles that separates German blood from German blood by artificial bounds must be broken.

2. Germany is overpopulated. She cannot feed her people from her own soil. The yearly rising surplus population faces the specter of hunger and starvation in a not far distant future.

3. New lebensraum must, therefore, be conquered—land that can be settled with German peasants. In this way Germany will become a healthy state, able to feed the nation without resort to foreign markets. Thus, freed from the dangers of a lopsided overindustrialized structure she can maintain a happy balance between agriculture and industry.

4. A radical program of racial eugenics will gradually restore to the German nation the pristine purity of the Nordic-Germanic blood. Among Germany's population the Nordics, that noblest group of that great noble Aryan family remains still dominant. Stop bastardization, purge the nation of its inferior stock, promote the Nordic blood—and Germany's strength will increase a thousandfold. Meanwhile the ironclad uniformity of Prussian militarism will give Germany national cohesion, will abate the disunity engendered by the lack of racial uniformity. Thus the march to world domination can start now.

5. Global conquest is not an end in itself. It is the means wherewith Germany fulfills a great "cultural mission" to make the world safe for the creative genius of the Aryan. For the history of culture is the history of the Aryan. By virtue of his intrinsic mental and moral superiority, the Aryan holds the top rank in the hierarchy of races. Today the biological purity of the Aryan is endangered all over the world.

The international Jew slyly prepares to rule the world. A Nordic Germany must act as the savior of the Aryan world.

6. By mating with bad stock the good stock is lowered. The half-breed loses his fitness to survive in the eternal struggle for existence. If he mixes with inferior races the Aryan squanders his precious biological heritage, his innate superiority. He flagrantly violates the will of nature to breed life towards a higher level.

7. Fundamental in nature is the aristocratic principle according to which mastery falls to the better and the stronger. But the right to mastery has to be validated by continuous struggle.

8. The "Creator" has given to the Germans the conditions, the opportunity, and the goals to bring about a greater cultural future. It is the duty of the Germans to fulfill their great mission. Racial purification and ruthless will to and use of power will be ways and means to bring salvation to the world by German rule.

The task that Hitler assigned to every German youth was to build a new Germany in the image of Nordic man, to build a race that was to make the world the sacred abode of Aryan culture. But before the new world could be built, the old, moribund world, afflicted with the sickly notions of pacifism, poisoned by democracy, and emasculated by humanitarian sentiment, had to be burned down. Germany's youth had to feel the moral grandeur of a noble mission. German youth had to learn to die not only for the good and the glory of Germany but also for the creation of a new world. War had to be fought as a holy war for the loftiest ideals. That spirit was to be the fuel that would drive the German war machine, the banner that in time to come would lead the regiments of Hitler's youth over the steppes of Asia and the deserts of Africa.

7 卐 The Power of an Idea on the Wane

The war went on. Hitler walked across Europe deep into Russia and Africa. In extending his power over continents Hitler used up his machinery, his natural resources, and above all, his labor reserves—presumably up to a crucial point. Thus today, officials and writers are seeking information and are speculating whether the Nazi grip on the German people is loosening. Stories brought over tell of signs of disintegration, clashes, even mutinies. Rumors of rebellious, bitter scenes taking place in the higher offices in Berlin and at headquarters between military officers and Nazis, between Hitler and his generals, may be well founded. Göring's ardent defense of Hitler's role in the Russian campaign corroborates such a surmise. Hitler's personal irresponsibility and incompetence in military matters are said to be discussed more frankly and anxiously in Nazi ranks. They are becoming apprehensive over the possible exhaustion of human and natural resources. The Russian campaign and the costly hibernation of the German troops in the eastern cold have deepened their worries. Not least, the entrance of the United States into the war reminded the older generation of what happened during the first world war—although this time Hitler and Goebbels declared war on the United States. Indubitably, the long-lasting war, starvation, and loss of life and property painfully affect every individual and every single family. It shakes millions of them into an awareness of what Hitler really did to them.

125

But all these indications of growing tension between the party and the army and the people, and among themselves, which leak out of Germany, do not permit the far-reaching conclusion that there is a serious sign of weakening war effort and sagging resistance. The disillusionment with Hitler and the Nazis and their invincibility is strongly compensated for by the fear the German people and the soldiers have of the results of another lost world war.

Middle-class people, murmuring and "yammering" among themselves in their sealed-up rooms, still cling fearfully to the Nazi war goals, cowering as they do before the Russian danger. Older military leaders in the army may heretically and openly discount the Nazi catechism as a collection of slogans, and even resist the permeation of their ranks with Nazi officers; yet actually they stand, as of yore, for discipline and fighting. The conservatives, full of hatred of Hitler because their great hope of using him as their tool was betrayed, are more than ever resolved to fight with him. And many fervent—and honest—patriots of liberal philosophy follow the Nazi flag for the good of their country in supreme danger. We know from eye-witnesses who have recently come from Europe that many businessmen, wounded officers, and soldiers have decided to turn their backs on Germany after the war—in utter contempt for the Nazi hell. But until then they will do their business and return to the front as disciplined fighters.

Nor is what we hear through recent information about the active and controlling Nazi column too optimistic for the Allied forces either. We may believe the stories that today, more than before the war, members of the Nazi party, the SS Guard, pay lip service to Hitler but have turned into hardened and frivolous opportunists. Yet there still remains an iron reserve of convinced followers whom the Nazi cynics call "German Idealists." Nor must we underrate the hundreds of thousands of faithful and enthusiastic youngsters who refill the iron reserve, carrying with them Hitler's war aims.

But even if the number of "true believers" shrink, and the number of opportunists grow greater within the Nazi organization, the opportunists and faithful adherents are chained together by destiny to uphold the Nazi control. It is obvious that the machine for the supervision of the territories has to be overloaded, and that the available forces, active adherents operating the machine, are thinning out. The Nazi control, as such, is not losing its grip, whether at home or on the far-flung frontiers. To make up for this attenuating process the Nazis have increased the strictness of their measures with regard to the defeatists at home and in the occupied areas. But more important—the growing difficulty of the task of holding together the totalitarian regime is, on the whole, facilitated by the help of the fear psychosis and the ardent support of the German patriots. Today German soldiers and the great majority of the people submit to Hitler without coercion and support him and his machine without belief, as long as they see in the defeat of nazism their own disaster and the entire destruction of Germany. Indeed, it is a paradoxical situation that Hitler needs less coercion today, because of less resistance to him. On the whole his control is made easier for him and is supplemented by voluntary control of the people. He can afford to permit grumbling within the broad, unpolitical strata since it does not grow dangerous.

On the other hand, Hitler and his ideology have definitely lost their appeal and influence among the compact mass that he formerly could call followers. Many of them are sick of Goebbels' voice. As we know from further analyses of the medium-wave broadcasts, the content of the Nazi propaganda has changed entirely. The war is no longer presented to the home front as a theater of efficiency and efficacy of victorious

German armies. The pictures have changed: the "Nazi truth" in motion pictures and radio appears to be replaced by the real truth of the bitter realities. The skillful touch of Goebbels is again apparent in the form of presentation of the new Nazi propaganda. In admitting the difficulties and in playing upon the fear psychosis, Goebbels tries, at the same time, to forestall complete desperation by telling German listeners and readers that the "Führer" had foreseen this period of hardship. In his present propaganda he sells the bitter realities as tactical detours which had been calculated in advance by the "Führer." Altogether the specific situation is no longer explained too frequently to the Germans under the aspects of the greater goals. Instead, propaganda is rather a threat than a prophecy and now utilizes the customary black-and-white method to impress upon the people the effects of a lost war. Not the ideas of Hitler are shown to the German people, but the results of defeat. Thus we can fairly judge that proportionately the numbers of disillusioned followers have increased, and the numbers of "enlightened" adherents have shrunk. Above all, the intercourse between his adherents and the mass no longer has the vitality, no longer possesses the revolutionary force that arose from the realization of the doctrine. The efficacy of inspiring the compact mass has decreased.

However, what we know from such individually collected bits of information leads us to assume that Hitler's police control of the German people through his organizations has not lessened. His power to drive armies into fighting is still strong. But Hitler and the Nazi power in Germany is greatly weakened and Hitler's final ideas fire fewer people in Germany and fewer adherents in his own organization. The German war effort is still strong, temporarily even rising, but the essential power of Hitler and the Nazi—that is, Hitlerism—is on the decline. The power of the idea is on the wane.

* * *

On the basis of our brief survey of the development of Hitlerism in Germany we shall be able to picture for ourselves what is going to happen in Germany. If our view of present-day Germany is correct, only a decisive military defeat can overthrow the Hitler system and break this mutually reenforcing alliance between the Germans of the past and the Hitlerites. What is going to happen after the defeat is rather beyond human imagination: when the volume of piled-up rage, when stalled and frustrated resistance will turn into the most bloody carnage ever witnessed in history. Lynching will be ubiquitous and everywhere Nazis will offer affidavits that they followed Hitler only under coercion.

Yet there will still be an iron reserve, perhaps split into small underground groups, particularly of younger Nazis, to keep alive the world of Hitler's ideas. We cannot guess their numerical strength. But even a few would be sufficient to reorganize larger cells once the first outbursts against national socialism have abated. Particularly those who abandon Hitler, without however finding new ideas or a new honest way of life, will still be prone to rejoin the Hitlerites. The world witnessed once, after 1918, how former ideals, represented at that time by the conservatives, gave in temporarily after the breakdown of Germany. But the same conservative "weltanschauung" soon recovered its strength, since true Republican-Democratic ideals never superseded Wilhelmian mentality. One reason for this failure was undoubtedly the mistaken method of liberal education applied to a breed accustomed to authoritarian rule; but more to be blamed were the facilities which the democracy liberally provided for the conservatives to reestablish their own organizations. Through them they freely spread their contempt for the Weimar Republic and thereby undermined its authority.

History once proved that an authoritarian cannot be transformed into a democrat by thoroughgoing democratic and liberal methods. He will, on the contrary, be more readily inclined to overthrow the democratic institutions and ideals by playing the democratic game. It would be irresponsibility on the part of the democratic peoples, were they to make the ill-fated attempt again to use their own methods and rules on objects even more unfit than Prussian authoritarians—namely the dictatorial Hitlerites. Only a people which has made the inner spirit of democracy its own, can govern itself at home and be handled democratically in the concert of peoples.

The task of rebuilding and fitting Germany into a new but more permanent peace is complicated by the problem that national socialism as well as fascism is not restricted to the country of its origin. There are warning signs throughout Europe that the folk ideology has soaked into the minds of younger and nationalistic peoples. These folk ideals grew out of the same roots as Hitlerism, although they may be less ambitious in political demands. They may have their own cast of nationalism, but they have similar justifications for "their" lebensraum.

The racial and "*Völkisch*-romantic" and anti-Semitic elements were merged by Hitler into a systematic unit and at the same time transformed into the far-reaching political program. In the tumult of war we do not like to be reminded that these elements of Hitler's system were not all of German origin only. To Hitler's *Weltbild* many of the European nations contributed ideologically, not least, French and English writers. The youth and the philosophers of all the nations are susceptible, above all, to such folk principles, which, in a highly political period, may again be formulated, as Hitler once did, into exaggerated nationalistic demands and rights, where the freedom and the value of the nation is deemed absolutely higher than the human rights of the individual. There is probable danger that nations in Europe will not only justify extreme nationalistic demands with folk ideas, but apply, in addition, totalitarian methods to maintain themselves as entities on a national basis. The totalitarian example of Hitler is especially attractive for those nations struggling with strong ethnic minorities.

*   *   *

To defeat Hitler demands a supreme military effort and a victory on the battlefields. But that alone would not result in winning the war. After a very short while the power of Fascist ideas in a starving and overpopulated Europe would reassert itself and become stronger than ever before—under different leaders. As Hitler and the Fascists once grew out of a mental atmosphere of despair in which neither the youngster nor the grown man could find guiding ideas and a final reason for life, so any hopeless European nation will be ridden by similar prophets and revolutionized by similar "messages."

To assure a durable peace the total eradication of the authoritarian and totalitarian ideas from Germany as well as from Europe is imperative. The problem of laying to rest Hitler's ghost leads to the discussion of European reconstruction. We shall abstain here from any general contribution to the plans of perhaps the greatest crusade of our century. In the context of our previous deliberations, we shall merely highlight some of the difficulties in the path of the reconstruction program.

We have to reconcile ourselves to the idea of a prolonged military occupation throughout Europe, a heavy burden for a country in which isolationism has been rampant again and again. Without military occupation a normal order of life cannot be established in Europe. But the occupation should not be restricted to such a policing task. More has to be done. Under the protective help of the military occupation social and economic cooperation of the peoples in Europe must be achieved. Without such a prolonged armistice the nationalistic aspirations of the various ambitious peoples will interfere again with economic recuperation and the betterment of the social conditions of the masses. During the first period of the shift from a wartime to a peace economy, a grandiose program of public works for the reconstruction of destroyed areas and for the replacement of worn-out industrial and transportation facilities must provide the basis for social security for the workers. Following this, Europe has to become accustomed to intra-European economic intercourse, providing the preconditions for great mass production for an increasing home market without the interference of protective and nationalistic tariff walls. A new division of labor will make for permanent political cooperation for European peoples, obliterating the importance of specific frontiers. A socioeconomic structure of Europe must be devised under which the peoples of Europe will learn to esteem the national state less than a European comity established under the higher law of human dignity and justice.

It should be emphasized that these high ideals have their own sociological climate in prosperity and increasing welfare of the peoples, while insecurity of the masses engenders a political atmosphere under which totalitarian fascism can readily sprout. The purification of Europe from totalitarianism is in the first instance an economic and social problem that can be solved only with the active participation and great material sacrifices of the Anglo-American countries.

An economic and political assimilation of European peoples is a difficult but realistic way to a new democratic Europe. Its difficulties and responsibilities cannot be taken over by the alternative palliatives of educating or reeducating and feeding European peoples from the outside. Fascist youth will not be impressed by clement generosity, even when supported by the so necessary distribution of food. It is the great tradition of our country to import culture by settling peoples from all over the world within our borders, merging them into the American way of life. But this example, great in history, does not permit the experiment of reexporting humanitarian ideals by visiting teachers without first having founded the social conditions ready to receive and develop them.

Under the new social circumstances the forces that harbor progressive and democratic potentialities can gradually infiltrate their spirit into the newly built social and political institutions, provided that these forces are given protection and, this time, international support. It should be emphasized that a new democracy for Europe cannot be a continuation of the old Weimar Republic, since the social structure of that time no longer exists. Nor can it be modeled after Anglo-Saxon institutions and concepts of law. It has to grow from within and has to be trained along lines which answer to the German's needs for abstract ideas, such as the concept of the *Rechtsstaat* and their sentiment for the essentially humanitarian principle of the right of protection for the weak.

Experience after the last war should have taught the democratic countries that after the armistice European armies cannot simply be demobilized and sent home. Officers and soldiers, together with former conservatives or Nazi iron reserves, must not again be permitted to form organizations under new disguised names but with old authoritarian and Fascist ideals. There is only one solution: that Nazis and Fascists all over Europe, particularly the younger ones, be kept in working camps in strict discipline and as groups—both modes of life to which they are habituated. In this way, labor troops can do useful work for the restoration of the destroyed areas. Native teachers, convinced of democratic ideas, but applying disciplinarian methods, may succeed very gradually in sifting out from the camps individuals who promise to cooperate in a new democratic community. It may be bitter for a man brought up in a humanitarian spirit to realize that a democratic order in Europe can be introduced only by military occupation and by the strict methods of authoritarianism; particularly to a larger part of European youth. But to arrive at this conclusion one must only have gained an insight into the mind and will of a young Nazi.

> Hans Staudinger
> New School for Social Research
> New York City
> 1944

Hans Staudinger

Biographical Afterword
Hans Staudinger, 1889–1980

Hans Staudinger was born in 1889 into an educated, Hessian, Protestant family and died peacefully in New York in February, 1980. His youth was shaped by the political and intellectual problems current in the last generation of the German empire. His father, Franz Staudinger, was an economist, teacher and "ethical" socialist who was close to both August Bebel and Ferdinand Tönnies. As a university student at Heidelberg, Staudinger joined the *Wandervogel*, organized a short-lived temperance union, and participated in a secret socialist student group to which his father and Emil Lederer (who would be his colleague in New York) also belonged. At eighty-nine Hans Staudinger insisted, "I was always a socialist. Your youth dreams, you know, must remain. I am still a socialist, one of the few who has the ideal of men living together in harmony, the best way possible. A real community."[1] That commitment remained steadfast throughout Staudinger's life.

As a young student, from his earliest days at Heidelberg University, Staudinger had taken an active part in the left-wing debate concerning the "social question," particularly in the critique of the orthodox Marxist prediction of imminent pauperization of the working class. The evolution of the Social Democratic Party (SPD) in Germany between 1890 and 1930 was in part based on the conviction that the material

1. Hans Staudinger, Interview I, November 1, 1978.

conditions of the working classes were improving, a process that in a democratic society eliminated the need for revolution.[2] In his university days, however, Staudinger still clung to an even more youthful vision of a spontaneous political community. His interest in creating such a community remained one of the central themes of his life.

It is not surprising that the "social question" was a subject of discussion between Staudinger and his teachers Alfred and Max Weber. At Heidelberg, Staudinger read for his doctorate in sociology and economics and developed his thesis under the supervision of Alfred Weber. Staudinger's contacts with Max Weber were, although informal, personally intense and remained so until the latter's death a decade later. Alfred Weber was his professor, Max Weber his teacher.

For the German intellectual of sixty years ago, Max Weber was a figure of enormous intellectual power and influence. Of the original members of the "University in Exile" at the New School for Social Research, almost half were trained in or influenced by Weberian sociology, though they represented several different disciplines in the social sciences. Staudinger was representative of that initial group. He was, seemingly, a Weberian, a socialist, a private scholar. These tensions played a prominent role in the choices he made as the author of *The Inner Nazi*. The ambivalence that it reveals, especially in his attempt to systematically understand the relationship between democracy, culture, and technological change, were unique neither to Staudinger nor to his European and American colleagues. They were the hallmark of Max Weber as well.

Staudinger considered Weber a cultural historian who sought to understand both past and present by the use of ideal types, methodological constructs that in recreating reality made it meaningful. Weber investigated the social, economic, and psychological parameters of human culture. His meth-

2. Staudinger to Hans Speier, April 10, 1978, in New School Archives.

odology posed enormous conceptual problems. Subsequent debates, for example, have focused on the nihilism inherent in the value-free discipline that Weber has been credited with creating. But Staudinger was not primarily concerned about whether reality could be objectified or understood in a way uninformed by present or subjective values. He interpreted Weber to imply that socialism, a value, was not derivable scientifically from historical data. It was a belief, a phenomenon, which could be explained culturally but whose validity was not scientifically verifiable. Both Staudinger and Weber agreed that Marx's science was neither predictive nor value free and therefore Weber's analysis of culture, of the evolution and development of bourgeois values, was at least for the present correct.[3] Weber identified the historical process of embourgeoisement (*Verburgerlichung*) rather than the dialectic of class struggle as the means by which European society had become rationalized, mechanical, and material. The original "calling" that had informed the ethic of capitalism, the resounding clanging of the monastery gate closing behind the emergence of "modern" values had become transformed into the "fate of our times . . . the disenchantment of the world."[4] While Weber insisted that this was an objective evaluation, in the *Protestant Ethic and the Spirit of Capitalism* with its anguished foretelling of "last men" caught in the "iron cage," he revealed a pessimistic cultural criticism. Contemporary culture was not merely materialistic but had outgrown the spiritual forces of its origins. In short, Weber arrived at a formulation of historical "laws" of process that the evolutionary socialist, no longer satisfied with the mechanics of Marxism, could accept in its analytical if not its critical form.

3. Staudinger, Interview I.
4. Max Weber, "Science as a Vocation," in H. H. Gerth and C. Wright Mills (trans. and eds.), *From Max Weber: Essays in Sociology* (New York: Oxford University Press, 1955), 154–55, 155.

Staudinger's Ph.D. thesis, published in 1913 as *The Individual and Community*, shared Weber's analysis of this "disenchantment," but unlike Weber's, Staudinger's conclusions were optimistic. Staudinger inquired into the social relationships within culture and the degree to which cultural values of the historical moment shaped the concept of the individual. The specific framework was the evolution of musical societies in Europe since the middle ages. Here he shared a historical conception with both Max and Alfred Weber. Staudinger contrasted the supposedly organic community of the middle ages with the apparently mechanized and authoritarian modern world. He sought to demonstrate the disintegration of the spiritual ethos of an earlier era and its replacement by modern individualism which was neither creative nor satisfying to the participating individual. As a cultural historian Staudinger saw any organization as an archetype of general society. "An organization is more than its people . . . it is a community, a small republic, and its rules are those of political behavior."[5] If the values of a particular moment contributed to the social and economic forms of the next, so these new social and economic forms must in turn create new cultural values.

This theory had important implications for Staudinger as a German socialist. It suggested that, although the German working class might improve its material condition, it would not adopt the cultural forms of the German bourgeoisie. Embourgoisement as an evolutionary process helped explain the failure of Marx's historical prognosis of a working-class socialist revolution, and Weber's rejection of a narrow economic understanding of class opened the way for the application of

---

5. Staudinger, *Individuum und Gemeinschaft in Der Kulturorganisation des Vereins* (Jena: E. Diederichs, 1913), 4. See also Alfred Weber's Introduction to *Individuum*, 3.

other factors in consideration of social stratification. Yet, for Staudinger, the working class as a class continued to exist. He believed that "rationalized" production combined with technological change offered the working class for the first time the opportunity to pursue, even create, "culture." Not only would the working class be liberated by economic prosperity, but Staudinger also believed, its cultural values would be shaped by the new industrial forms. "The world of the workers," he wrote, "is best compared to a spring tap: it creates its economic surroundings." Working class organizations, musical societies in this case, were small republics, and like those of the middle ages they stressed the value of the collectivity, of the community. In the world of the worker the "exaltation of the individual no longer exists."[6]

Staudinger concluded that if contemporary culture was at odds with its collectivist economic forms it was because its values failed to interpret modern reality accurately. Art, for Staudinger, derived meaning from the human community it was created to serve. The appearance of music societies within the working class reaffirmed that the "masses," when liberated, might truly create. The crux of Staudinger's analysis rested on his understanding of the liberating and creative prospects of leisure time. The emergence of a working class culture would put an end to the highly subjective and individualistic character of modern art and culture. In retrospect Europeans would view the contemporary obsession with personality "as an episode during which a wonderful epoch became static in its lack of focus."[7] Paradoxically, the individual ethic of capitalism created a structurally collectivized society, which in turn gave rise to a communitarian culture that repudiated the excessive individualism that Staudinger believed

6. Staudinger, *Individuum*, 171.
7. *Ibid.*, 172.

characterized capitalism and modern culture. As a result the working class culture would emerge as a result not of revolution, but of the historical process that was inherent in the modern world. In Weber, Staudinger found the historical justification of his social-democratic beliefs.

Staudinger's education as a student of Weber had been characterized by a series of exchanges between two men. Although Weber's ideas had a significant imprint on the young civil servant and socialist, Staudinger refused full discipleship. In fact, his service to the Prussian state bureaucracy seemed a betrayal of Weber's principles. For Weber bureaucracies embodied the depersonalized rationalizaion that stifled creativity. Bureaucracies, for Weber, in public or corporate form, represented the ultimate dead end of capitalism which he described as the "iron cage." But Staudinger, less pessimistic than his mentor, believed that through politics, specifically democratic socialism, rationalized economic structures could lead to fulfilling and creative cultural forms rather than depersonalized and static institutions. Only as a socialist politician could his dream of an industrial, democratic community be realized.

In contrast, Weber argued that in the democratic age the state could not be created anew by conventional politicians, it could merely be contended for. Only a true prophet could reconstitute the state, although Weber asserted that such a prophet "simply does not exist."[8] Yet, clearly the "iron laws" of the democratic present that rendered real or charismatic leadership and, thus, revolution impossible did not make the belief in charismatic leaders unimaginable.

Contemporary existence was rational and material, the result of a cultural process of secularization. In Weber's analysis

8. Weber, "Science as a Vocation," 153.

this secular life limited the very spirit of culture that it could in turn create. Similarly, the process by which the "political" had become administrative meant for Weber that the "political administrator" could no longer do precisely what "the politician must always do . . . namely fight." For "to take a stand, to be passionate . . . is above all the element of the political leader." Thus, while the civil servant administered in the name of the state that he served and was responsible to that organization, the "real politician," who knew power, acted in his own name. "The honor of the political leader, of the leading statesmen . . . lies precisely in an exclusive *personal* responsibility for what he does." To seek after this knowledge and responsibility was to invite disaster. Weber offered little consolation for those committed to conventional political solutions. "Not a summer's bloom lies ahead of us," he prophesied, "but rather a polar night of icy darkness."[9]

Weber's essays on science and politics bisected these worlds into distinct spheres. The limits imposed by his understanding of the modern world were parallel. The politician and the scientist, who were to be concerned with different aspects of the same question—the role of values in political communities—were no longer "free" to act or to guide action. Staudinger accepted Weber's notion of the distinctness of the two spheres. As a socialist he devoted himself to the political, and as a politician he understood the meaning of personal responsibility. That responsibility, however, entailed a knowledge of the values that informed his political activity. Trained as a social scientist, Staudinger continued to view his world in political terms. Even as Staudinger rejected Weber's pessimistic judgment on modern culture, he likewise steered clear of Weber's extreme political alternatives of a stagnant bu-

9. *Ibid.*, 95, 128.

reaucracy or charismatic leader. Instead Staudinger sought, through politics, to use his skills and knowledge to make Germany a socialist democracy.

His studies terminated, Staudinger entered the German army shortly after the outbreak of World War I. In 1916 and 1917 he fought on the front lines and was twice decorated for bravery and twice wounded. During the war, Staudinger came into contact with socialists and trade unionists who assumed leadership of postwar Germany. Staudinger also continued to see Weber, who apparently approved Staudinger's growing interest in politics. Increasingly, Staudinger appreciated that, despite Weber's claim to value-free social science, Weber was nevertheless committed to the German state.[10] His scholarly pronouncements notwithstanding Weber's real passion was politics. Staudinger in some way represented Weber's ideal of the politician, not as a prophet, but as one whose "calling" corresponded to the man who lived "for politics," who served the state.

By the summer of 1918, both the German General Staff and the Socialist party were aware of Germany's inevitable military defeat.[11] The SPD asked Staudinger to prepare the soldiers and unionists with whom he was in contact for that defeat and for, presumably, their political support in the new socialist Germany that would emerge at war's end. At the same time, Weber asked Staudinger to send special advice to Friedrich Ebert, advice that Staudinger found remarkably naïve for a man whose concern was so intensely political. Moderate socialists wanted to stave off the Marxist revolution that the followers of Rosa Luxemburg and Karl Liebknecht

10. Staudinger, "Memoir on Weber" (manuscript dated 1976 in New School Archives); Staudinger, Interview IV, December 22, 1978.
11. Adolph Lowe, Interview, February, 1979; Staudinger, Interview III, December 18, 1978.

hoped to foment. At this critical moment, Weber advised a complete rupture between the SPD and the military.[12] As a supporter of the Social Democratic position, which considered an alliance with the military critical to the establishment of political democracy, Staudinger severed his relationship with Weber.

In the spring of 1919, Hans Staudinger received his appointment with the title of *Geheimrat* in the Reich's Ministry of Economics. He was one of only three bureaucrats to receive this title, which conferred aristocratic status, before it was discontinued. Staudinger served as the administrative adjutant for general political matters in liaison with the trade unions.[13] A member of the Social Democratic party, he remained in this position, directly below that of state secretary, until 1927, serving ministers whose political positions became increasingly at odds with his own. Staudinger's own political and intellectual evolution during the Weimar years mirrored the history of his times. After 1927 he abandoned the Reich for Prussia, and following the "Papen Putsch" in the summer of 1932, which obliterated Germany's federal structure, he left political administration to become an intransigent socialist member of the Reichstag. Initially, however, two events forced Staudinger to sharpen his economic and political views. The failure of the Socialization Commission in 1918–1919 to achieve a nationalized economy was followed by the challenge of conservative reaction in the form of the Kapp Putsch in the spring of 1920. The German socialist movement having already quashed its revolutionary left wing found itself with few alternatives in the wake of these developments. Consequently, Staudinger supported the position ad-

12. Staudinger, Interview IV.
13. See also Arnold Brecht, *The Political Education of Arnold Brecht: An Autobiography* (Princeton: Princeton University Press, 1971), 163.

vocated by Walther Rathenau.[14] Rather than return to the idea of socializing the means of production, Staudinger agreed with Rathenau, Wichard von Möllendorff, and his New School colleague Adolph Lowe that a socialist economy and a socialist community, a *Gemeinwirtschaft*, could be built within the existing political and economic order. He committed himself to the state-capitalism or planned economy that Rathenau and others supported. Given the increasingly difficult split between the unions and the SPD, the adoption of *Planwirtschaft*, or state-as-entrepreneur policy, seemed a viable "socialist" alternative to Staudinger. He could embrace it both as a member of the SPD and as a state bureaucrat.

Staudinger's socialism matched his revised understanding of Weber's teaching. As an administrative politician, Staudinger discovered, especially during the Kapp Putsch, that he had a role to play in decision-making that clearly transcended the limits that Weber had argued modern society imposed on politicians. When the cabinet fled Berlin for Stuttgart in March of 1920, and with his minister in touch only irregularly by telephone, Staudinger found that he had important political decisions to make concerning food and provisions as the Berlin general strike evolved. "I closed the milk deliveries to the city and advised the workers to go on strike . . . all in the name of my minister." Subsequently Robert Schmidt, Staudinger's minister, told an inquiry that Staudinger had acted in his name. Staudinger recognized the limits of Weberian ideal-type characterizations. "Weber had no flesh and blood in his understanding. I was an administrative bureaucrat who had a

14. Lowe interview. See also W. F. Bruck, *Social and Economic History of Germany from William II to Hitler, 1888–1938: A Comparative Study* (Oxford: Oxford University Press, 1938), particularly 143–98. Bruck credits Möllendorff with the invention of the term *Planwirtschaft*, which Staudinger saw as the means to a *Gemeinwirtschaft*, an economic community, an "organized economy."

great deal of political discretion, not just in the emergency of the Kapp Putsch, but in day to day operations as well."[15] Here Staudinger came to appreciate the degree to which skill and adroitness importantly affected political decision-making. The choice for him included alternatives other than those of prophecy and bureaucracy.

Committed to a program of economic planning as a practical means of creating socialism, Staudinger by the mid 1920s recognized that German conservatives had begun to succeed where the Kapp Putsch had failed. The personnel of the imperial German bureaucracy also staffed the Reich bureaucracy. At the same time the SPD found itself excluded from the governing Weimar "coalition." Their base crumbling and their leadership divided, Social Democrats turned to their last stronghold, the state government of Prussia. In 1927 Staudinger had few reasons to regret his forced transfer to Prussia.

The Prussian state under Minister-President Otto Braun, a Social Democrat, was a fertile ground for Staudinger's political and economic gifts and socialist convictions. Giving up the battle to make the Reich government an entrepreneur, Staudinger found in Prussia a state government with extensive publicly owned industries. With the title of state secretary in the Prussian Ministry of Trade and Commerce, Staudinger coordinated the entire energy industry of the government: electricity, ore, potash. He combined electrical companies into the Allgemeine Deutsche Elektrizitätswirtschaft, reduced prices, and represented Prussia in the *Reichsrat*. In 1931 he and several colleagues not only protested the Brunning government's deflationary economic and fiscal response to the depression, but also presented a wide-ranging program for reform. Although the German government did not adopt these proposals, the

15. Gordon A. Craig, *Germany, 1866–1945* (New York: Oxford University Press, 1978), 420–31; Staudinger, Interview III, IV.

Prussian state government, under Staudinger's guidance, followed an essentially Keynesian economic path in 1931 and 1932. To stimulate consumption and reduce unemployment, Staudinger and his colleagues in the Prussian bureaucracy used profits from their state industries to finance public works programs, which in turn provided employment and income for unemployed workers. Staudinger's contention that Prussian economic recovery had its first noticeable effect just at the moment of the "Papen Putsch" is borne out by contemporary and recent economic studies.[16]

The effort by Staudinger and others to create a socialist "organized economy" by transforming private cartels into state enterprises was stopped in its tracks by the Reich government. On July 20, 1932, German Prime Minister Franz von Papen dissolved the Prussian government of Otto Braun, ending the historic tension of German-Prussian dualism and in the process eliminating Prussia's independent economic policy. Staudinger's future colleague in New York, Arnold Brecht, who also had joined Braun in 1927, went on to successfully challenge the legality of the coup before the German supreme court. Staudinger, however, chose to declare his candidacy for the Reichstag from Hamburg.[17]

As a "young socialist" committed to the maintenance of the party even as an underground political organization, Staudinger embraced the general slogan of the party, "Hitler means war," and won a seat in the Reichstag. Almost overnight he moved from the confines of the ministry into the

16. W. Hagen-Schutze, *Otto Braun* (Frankfurt: Propyläen, 1978); Brecht, *Political Education*, 322; Staudinger, Interview V, January 3, 1979; Gustav Stolper, *The German Economy, 1870 to the Present* (2nd ed.; New York: Harcourt, Brace, and World, 1967), 118. See also the report of Société Financière de Transports et d'Entreprises Industrielles, *Memorandum on New Business Development in the Electric Light and Power Industry in Germany, 1932–1936* (Brussels: Government of Belgium, October 1, 1938), 2.

17. Hamburg was the scene of great turbulence and electoral violence in July, 1932.

hectic and violent world of German partisan politics. His adherence to the program of continued and, if necessary, clandestine socialist activity gained his reelection in November and brought the enmity of the opposition, Nazi and Communist. In early 1933 he recalls narrowly escaping an assassination attempt by so-called Communist squads who one evening waited for him to cross the Elbe by ferry. His closest assistant, a Communist infiltrator, tipped him off at the last moment, "Don't take the ferry tonight." What the Communists failed to accomplish, the Nazis almost achieved. In April, 1933, within weeks of Hitler's appointment as chancellor, Staudinger was arrested at a meeting of his socialist group for defying the ban on political activity. At the time he had been entrusted with more than a million marks, which he had raised from the Berlin banker Otto Jeidels, who may have been representing the *Centralverein*, the major assimilationist organization of German Jewry. Jeidels had given Staudinger the money specifically for the Socialist party to expose the anti-Semitism of the National Socialist program.[18]

Staudinger remembers being, at the time, almost alone in interpreting Nazi political doctrine as embodying the ideological pronouncements contained in *Mein Kampf*. His socialist colleagues, like Rudolph Hilferding, regarded the book as monstrous drivel and could not bring themselves to read it, while Jewish friends and associates, especially anti-Zionists, in 1931 refused his appeal for an anti-Nazi, antiracist fund in the Socialist party.[19] Staudinger, along with Carlo Mierendorff, had been the spiritual and political leader of the Young Socialists. Of the thirty-six in their clandestine group, all but one were arrested in 1933 by the Reich Police. Of those captured only Staudinger was charged with treason and threatened with hanging. After six weeks of intermittent beatings,

18. Staudinger, Interview V, VI (February, 1979).
19. *Ibid.*

solitary confinement, and secret messages to his lawyer and wife, Staudinger found out that his million marks were safe and he would be released. As a result of his wife's efforts the king of Belgium intervened on his behalf. In June, 1933, he was permitted to leave on the conditions that he never appear again in Hamburg but that he report back in September. Failure to meet these conditions would result in the rearrest of his thirty-six colleagues.

In the fall of 1933 Hans Staudinger was in exile. "Of all of us, you know," said one of his colleagues at the New School, "Staudinger paid the dearest. They were very brutal with him. He earned his passage and our respect." The faculty that Staudinger joined in 1934 had been created by Alvin Johnson, President of the New School for Social Research, and Emil Lederer, the first dean of the University in Exile. Lederer and Staudinger had known each other as early as 1911 when they had both been young "secret" socialists at Heidelberg. In London in the spring of 1933 Johnson and Lederer hammered out a list of individuals whom they intended to extend invitations to join the faculty. As Johnson later explained, "I didn't set up a University in Exile just to create an island of security for a small group of scholars, but as a challenge to the university world to show that it knew of its responsibility to persecuted merit."[20]

Hans Staudinger was forty-three when he joined the New School faculty. He had turned down offers to work for the Turkish and Belgian governments. It seemed that he had chosen to abandon politics for science. In fact, politics continued to dominate his work as a social scientist at the New School. The climate that he found and that engaged his political inter-

20. Erich Hula, Interview, October 15, 1978; Hans Speier, Interview, April, 1979. Speier, sent by Johnson and Lederer to recruit a faculty in Germany, also met Staudinger at Lederer's house. Alvin Johnson to Else Staudinger, May 8, 1965, in New School Archives.

est was embodied by the New Deal and by Johnson's declaration that in "America there is social change in the making." Staudinger's initial concern in the 1930s was to build a distinguished faculty, promote his statist ideas, and avoid being misrepresented. "My students never seemed to understand when I talked of economic community, of an organized, planned economic arrangement in which political democracy was but the first step in establishing social democracy."[21] In the United States, Staudinger had great difficulty conveying his economic and political ideas. His writing of *The Inner Nazi* can be seen as an effort to communicate his concerns, and his refusal to publish it, a consequence of his fear of being misunderstood.

Staudinger's major impact on the New School was as a leader. His colleagues turned to him in the midst of their weekly battles, and the school itself turned to him for help with its perennial financial crises.[22] Repeatedly he raised important sums, and he obtained the funding for the Institute of World Affairs, a research group that provided support for numerous European exiles. Under the leadership of Staudinger's friend and colleague Adolph Lowe, the institute, a prototype for postwar "think tanks," sponsored studies on totalitarianism, radio propaganda, and economic forecasting and provided the intellectual environment in which *The Inner Nazi* (1944) and the other project that Staudinger initiated, the Leisure-Time Study, were developed.

The Leisure-Time Study was an extension of the work Staudinger had begun under Max and Alfred Weber. Staudinger sought to understand the relationship between culture, society, and democracy. "The cultural pattern of our society has undergone changes," Staudinger wrote. "What we do not un-

21. Johnson to Else Staudinger, May 8, 1965, in New School Archives; Jehuda Riemer, Interview, July 25, 1978.
22. Hula, Interview; Staudinger, Interview II.

derstand yet is the direction. . . . These changes are revolutionary, and the transition to mass culture is still in flux." Specifically, Staudinger hoped to identify the relation of these changes to the working classes. He recalled his own earlier work and optimism: "I believed then that the individual and group relationship as developed in the workers' associations was becoming typical for an ever increasing part of society, and that *in the coming age of the organized masses, similar to the Middle Ages, the pattern of life, evolving from new values would be guided by the universally recognized dogmas.*" Staudinger wanted to reaffirm the optimism of his youth in postwar American society. He believed that "culture founded on a high degree of individualism . . . was destined to be only an historical episode." He also believed that these were questions of moment for the stability of democratic societies. He remained steadfast in his commitment to socialism. "As I have said before, modern democracy must be founded on social democracy." Staudinger hoped to determine the nature of working class "cultural" activity in American society, since culture is "the sphere of activities devoted to perceiving and understanding the inner sense of mankind and the world."[23] For him economic well-being unaccompanied by cultural refinement did not represent social progress. By *culture* Staudinger did not mean the shared values of a group, but rather social refinement. By studying the use of leisure time by American workers he hoped to demonstrate the validity of democracy.

Staudinger based his study on the assumption that the workplace influenced workers' values more than other factors such as the home or religion. Through elaborate polls and interviews he tried to determine if workers derived long-term

23. Staudinger to Lowe, January 16, 1948, Staudinger, "Leisure-Time and Free-Time Studies" (note, research materials, and prospectus), both in New School Archives.

"satisfaction" as well as short-term "pleasure" from their leisure-time activities. He concluded that, while immediate "pleasure" was high, long-term "satisfaction" was low. That is, American workers seemed to enjoy themselves in their off-hours, but they failed to use their leisure to increase their "cultural refinement." For Staudinger this seemed a serious indictment of working-class culture and at odds with his life-long correlation of social democracy and cultural progress. Finding the results at odds with his political beliefs, Staudinger chose not to publish his conclusions. As in 1944 with *The Inner Nazi*, Staudinger in 1948 preferred to remain unpublished rather than commit to print anything that might damage political causes in which he believed.

In contrast to the leisure study, *The Inner Nazi* contains little of the apparatus of a social scientist. It was not necessary for Staudinger and his assistant Werner Pese to question the nature or the method of the phenomenon that they were explaining. Nazism was most importantly a political movement of extraordinary ideological power. It was necessary to recognize that racism and the policy of expansion to the east were at the core of nazism. The rediscovery of *The Inner Nazi* allows us to recognize the verity of Staudinger's political evaluation. As a man of politics and political action, he knew and appreciated his enemies in ways that many of his contemporaries could or would not admit. His decision not to publish the manuscript was based on this knowledge and judgment. The enemy was, finally, not modern society, but those who wanted to destroy it.

Peter M. Rutkoff
William B. Scott
Gambier, Ohio
1980